How to Become a Caterer

Everything You Need to Know From Finding Clients to the Final Bill

Susan Wright

The Learning Series

A Citadel Press Book
Published by Carol Publishing Group

Copyright © 1996 Susan Wright

A Citadel Press Book
Published by Carol Publishing Group
Citadel Press is a registered trademark of Carol Communications, Inc.
Editorial, sales and distribution, rights and permissions inquiries should be addressed to Carol Publishing Group, 120 Enterprise Avenue, Secaucus, N.J. 07094
In Canada: Canadian Manda Group, One Atlantic Avenue, Suite 105, Toronto, Ontario M6K 3E7

Carol Publishing Group books may be purchased in bulk at special discounts for sales promotion, fund-raising, or educational purposes. Special editions can be created to specifications. For details, contact Special Sales Department, 120 Enterprise Avenue, Secaucus, N.J. 07094.

Manufactured in the United States of America
10 9 8 7 6 5 4 3 2 1

Library of Congress Cataloging-in-Publication Data

Wright, Susan.
    How to become a caterer : everything you need to know from finding clients to the final bill / Susan Wright.
        p. cm.
    ISBN 0–8065–1827–8 (pbk.)
    1. Caterers and catering. I. Title.
TX911.2.W735 1996
642'.4—dc20
                                                    96–28043
                                                         CIP

Contents

Foreword

by Kelly Beaton

If you have a basic knowledge of the service industry and food preparation, you can become a caterer. I started out by cooking in restaurants for several years. Then a frantic friend called and said she needed someone to carve meat at a Christmas party. I said sure, I can carve meat.

From that moment on, I learned the catering business the hard way—by doing the jobs and making the mistakes. After twelve years in the catering and restaurant businesses (primarily at the Party Source in Syracuse, Florent in New York City, and Pastabilities in Syracuse), I realized that a catered function was organized according to a simple set of service rules for the various types of meals and events. You'll find those guidelines in this book; the rest is creativity and common sense.

On my first job I discovered the basic principle of catering: Make the food look good. I didn't know what I was doing, but wearing a white chef's coat with woven frogs made me look like a pro. And when the guests constantly commented on the appearance of the meat, I put a bus tub under the table and kept the board scraped clean so the only thing they saw was the juicy chunk of roast beef being slowly and deliberately sliced.

The appearance of your meals will determine the success of your business. If the food looks good, people will be complimentary even if the flavors are not to everyone's taste. But if the presentation is sloppy or displeasing, the guests will complain that the food is bad.

It's been my experience that the easiest way to start a catering business is to work with a local restaurant that already has cooking facilities, serving supplies, and distribution contacts. Customers tend to ask their favorite restaurants for special dishes for their private parties anyway, and many restaurants are perfectly aware of the desirability of their food even though they don't have the time or ability to set up a sideline catering business.

If you don't have a restaurant to work with, all you need is a large kitchen and some initiative. Hiring and training both kitchen and service staff is easy. Wages are low, and the work is part-time so you don't have to worry about insurance and benefits.

Aside from the catering manager, the most important employee is your chef. The chef is responsible for purchasing quality food and preparing it with flair. Prices must be kept down, while the spread has to look as though it was made for royalty. Your chef must be able to meet the creative challenges involved in making the food look complex and attractive, while keeping the menus simple and easy to prepare.

For the most part, your clients will want the basics when it comes to food. They also want familiarity—if the food served is unusual, the guests may be put off by it and they won't like anything. Sticking to the common denominator will also make it easier for your kitchen staff to prepare menus. It's best to offer a core selection of items, along with a few unique dishes.

When your business is first starting, you may have to take a cut on the profits in order to build up a base clientele. You can do this by offering incentives in the form of extras, like a special salad included without charge, or two choices of desserts.

But for some clients, you'll find that nothing is enough, and they will start to *expect* that little extra as part of what they get for their money: With every job they ask for more. Clients who usually do this are the ones who throw parties on a regular basis, and they offer their next party to you as leverage to get a better deal. For example, they may want you to provide the plates, when the contract calls only for food, or they ask you to bring an extra flower arrangement for the entrance table.

It can be easy to get drawn into a never-ending cycle of giving more and more while the price remains the same. Your job is to please your client, but the bottom line must always be kept in mind. In one way, this sort of bargaining is what gives new caterers a chance to break into the business.

Organizing a function may seem like a daunting job, but this book makes it easier by breaking down every aspect of catering, from ordering food and renting serviceware to transportation and the actual running of the event. Whether the function is held in the client's home or in a rented hall, the quality of your food and service will attract new clients. This means that your work will be your advertising.

As your business grows, you'll have the satisfaction of really getting to know your clients while you help them celebrate the most memorable events in their lives. And with every function you cater, you will get new ideas from your clients. They know their guests, and their suggestions can often serve as the basis for your presentation.

During the function itself, it is up to the catering manager to strike the right balance between the service staff and the guests. One of my favorite functions was the annual Christmas delivery to the local public television station. While the rest of the employees had their Christmas party somewhere else, a skeleton crew stayed behind to run the station and have their own miniparty. The night manager of the station always ordered four or five extra meals because he liked having extra shrimp cocktails and desserts.

The first time I catered that party, the manager asked our staff to sit down and join them. I said we couldn't because we were working. Then we tried to stay over to one side of the room, but I realized that it was making the crew uncomfortable to have us hovering. We ended up joining them, and the next year, I didn't hesitate when the manager asked us to sit down. For that situation, it was the best thing we could have done, and the station manager kept using our catering business.

As catering manager you have to pay attention to the needs of the client, yet it is your responsibility to organize the staff and run the mechanical aspects of the event so the hosts have the freedom to devote their time to the guests.

I once worked for a hostess, the wife of a professor at Syracuse University, who threw very nice, private parties for professors and administrators in her husband's department. One party I arranged for her was in the spring, when the weather could sometimes be bad, so everything was set up inside the house. But as the party started, the guests were acting stiff and awkward. I realized that half of them were visiting German professors and their English was sketchy.

Since the sun was still out and the garden looked beautiful, I suggested that we open the doors and move some things onto the patio. The hostess didn't take kindly to the idea—she was afraid it wouldn't look good to change things after the party was started.

As catering manager for that function, I was responsible for creating a setting that would make the party a success. I ordered the staff to move the table outside despite the fact that it was against her wishes. As soon as things were moved, the professors were able to wander around and they stopped feeling trapped. Everyone relaxed, and the hostess was grateful in the end that I had taken control.

Being a catering manager is always exciting because no

two functions are alike. Yet even the most difficult and complex functions are easy once you know the tricks involved. Take surprise parties—they usually work if you make sure the client openly plans for something smaller to happen, such as a dinner foursome that has no pretense of being a surprise.

Yet you have to be prepared for even the best-laid plans to go awry. One client sent his wife out shopping so that the catering staff could set up a surprise birthday party for her. The guests were already waiting when she called to say she was going to be a couple of hours longer than she thought. The host had to innocently agree in order not to tip her off.

We made it work to our advantage and got the party going without her. It gave everyone something to talk about, planning for where they would hide and anticipating her reaction. The party was a success even before the birthday girl got home.

The catering manager can rescue even the worst situations, as long as he can maintain the illusion of control, assuring the client that everything will be taken care of. If something breaks, you have someone clean it up quickly and calmly instead of making a fuss. You make sure anything unpleasant is put out of sight and out of mind as quickly as possible.

The worst thing a catering manager has to deal with (aside from delivery delays) are food disasters. Early in my catering career, I was helping another person carry a six-foot sub out of the van. The sub was sitting on paper on a long plank and it slid right off. Now without thinking, we both looked around and saw that no one had seen it. So we put it back on the board and ran into the kitchen to clean it off and put everything back together.

Of course, food disasters usually happen right in front of the hosts or the guests, as was the case with the young woman who was carrying a turkey into a house for a private party. In full view of everyone, it slid off the platter and landed on the tile floor of the kitchen. We all froze (the hosts included), but the catering manager said ever-so-coolly, "Oh, just take that back out and get the other one." I almost believed it myself.

Sometimes food self-destructs. Usually it's helped along by one of your catering staff. Once, as we were doing the final prep at the banquet site, a young kitchen helper threw a whole, cooked lobster at a server. The lobster hit the wall and exploded. We practically flew to the nearest super-market to buy another lobster, and I thought we were going to have to cook it right then and there, but we managed to find one that was already prepared.

We weren't so lucky with the roasted pig for the barbecue party for the local police department. That time it was the fault of the food purchaser who ordered the pig and the skewers for the party. The skewers were too small, but the catering staff had to do their best to hold the pig up with them. Thankfully it had already been cooked, but the pig was so big that it wouldn't turn. It just hung there, the belly drooping in the fire, dripping fat.

It didn't take long before the flames leapt up and the pig caught on fire. Before we could put it out, it broke in half and the entire thing fell onto the ground. One guy was hitting it with his knife trying to put out the fire, while the cops sat around drinking their beer. They ate the part that landed up.

I've always liked that catering story the best because it sums up everything about the business. Your pig can land on the ground, but if you take it in stride they'll always eat the side that lands up.

Good luck with your catering business—it's one of the best ways you can earn money and have fun at the same time.

How to Become
a Caterer

1 | *Starting Your Own Catering Business*

Catering is one of the most risk-free, high-profit business ventures you can try. Whether you've got experience in the food industry or not, you can start and run your own catering business.

The initial investment for an off-premises catering business is comparatively low. The catering kitchen and the most basic equipment are all you will need to finance. Almost everything else, from linen to flatware to transport vans, can be rented on a per-function basis.

Each function is contracted for a specified number of guests, thereby eliminating waste when it comes to purchasing and preparing the meals. By contracting your services in advance, you are able to calculate to the penny what your profit will be for every function.

The client also pays a large deposit the day the contract is signed, which is nonrefundable if the job is canceled. You can use the deposit to pay for equipment rentals, food purchasing, and part-time prep help. And you don't have to worry about delayed payments—the balance of the total price is usually paid on the day of the function.

Your chef, salesperson, and banquet manager should be skilled at their jobs, but the service personnel and kitchen help can be unskilled labor. With most of your labor working part-time, you won't have to pay high payroll taxes, and the hourly wages are usually low.

At first, your business needs to cater only a few types of functions—for example, private formal dinners or children's birthday parties. This will make advertising, purchasing, and production much easier until your business is ready to expand.

Each time you cater a function, you are basically advertising to every guest who is present. This will inevitably lead to additional clients. Your catering business can grow on client demand until you are eventually producing wedding receptions and trade shows for hundreds of guests—perhaps even purchasing your own banquet facilities. This means that expansion (one of the deadly traps of small businesses) is done in manageable stages.

All you have to do is follow these easy steps, and your catering business will take off, taking you along with it for fun and profit.

Off-Premises Catering

An off-premises caterer can serve anything from a simple hors d'oeuvre platter to an elaborate formal wedding. The location is chosen by the client (either their home or a rented facility) or the caterer can be referred to clients by hotels, banquet halls, and other public function spaces that don't have on-staff catering.

Many caterers start their business by doing off-premises catering, and some continue even after they have purchased their own banquet facility. With off-premises catering, the food is prepared in the catering kitchen (your full-time business location), then is transported to the site of the function.

Most banquet facilities have a well-equipped kitchen that can be used, or your staff can set up a kitchen to finish the preparation and heating of the food before it is served.

Locations

When dealing with off-premise locations, your banquet manager or salesperson must survey the site before agreeing to the price of each function. You'll need to make sure the location is large enough and well-suited to the type of function the client wants to host.

What if a client has her heart set on getting married in her parents' garden, and you arrange all the details only to find that there's not enough banquet space for the number of guests? Then the client must either scale down the size of the function, or locate another space. Either way, by checking the feasibility of the location first, you've saved yourself the time and expense of planning a wedding reception that could never take place.

At each location, you'll have to assess the banquet space, cocktail area, and locations for things like dance floor, bars, and band area. You'll also have to check parking facilities, lighting, entrances and exits. The quality of the bathrooms is very important, and there must be enough to adequately serve the number of guests that will be invited.

Kitchen

You'll need to check the kitchen to make sure there's enough oven and refrigerator space and storage facilities. You also have to check the dishwashing facilities, electrical and gas hookups, and water supply to make sure the location can be used.

In some cases, you may have to adjust your menu to the site to ensure easier food preparation and service. Or additional equipment can be rented and set up: portable stoves (propane or canned heat), warming cabinets, and insulated coolers.

If the kitchen is set up near the same area as the banquet tables, you should hide the food preparation from the guests. Folding screens can be placed in front of the preparation tables and dishwashing facilities, or you can use a separate tent for the kitchen, or even set up in the garage.

Personnel

There are seven management duties involved in catering a function. Depending on the size of your business, one person can handle several of the departments for each function. For example, if your business has been contracted to cater an engagement party for forty people at the home of the bride's parents, you might have one person handle the duties of salesperson and production manager before the event, then act as the headwaiter at the function.

The duties of a catering business can be broken down as follows:

1. *The Banquet Manager*
   This person coordinates the catering staff in preparing the food and executing the function from start to finish. Depending on the size of the function, he can assume various roles such as menu planner for your business and production manager for each event, and act as headwaiter at the functions. But the primary duty of the banquet manager is to make sure all of the jobs are getting done.
2. *The Salesperson*
   This person makes contact with the client (including advertising and promotion), and gets all of the contract specifications for each function. The salesperson must make sure your business can provide what the client has ordered—whether it's a fifty-by-seventy-five-foot tent and a baked Alaska for dessert, or pony rides at a birthday

party. The rest of the catering staff works from the detailed contract which is signed by the client.

3. *The Menu Planner*
To create menus for your business, you must work closely with the chef. The chef breaks down the ingredients of each recipe so the food can be purchased in the proper amounts, and priced per person. The menu planner either does or delegates the purchasing, receiving, and storage of the food and liquor for each function.

4. *The Production Manager*
You will have to order the proper amount of linen, serviceware, and furniture for each function. The production manager must do comparison shopping to make sure your business is getting the best deals from local suppliers. The production manager also hires employees, and arranges the outside services such as flowers, photographer, entertainment, and printed materials.

5. *The Chef*
Your chef must be creative and economical in creating recipes and menus for your business. The chef oversees the preparation of the food prior to and during the function, and supervises the packing and transportation of the food.

6. *The Headwaiter*
The headwaiter arranges the layout of the rooms and conducts the function from setup to breakdown, delegating responsibilities to service personnel.

7. *Administration*
This is the nuts and bolts of your business—handling the details of running your permanent business location and catering kitchen. This is also where menu pricing and contracts are

finalized, depending on the cost of all aspects of
the business: food, labor, rental, overhead, etc.

The Banquet Manager

The banquet manager must consider each stage of the
function from beginning to end, taking into account the
budget and location. The banquet manager also delegates
the duties involved in each function, and prepares a
schedule to ensure everything gets done when it should. For
example:

1. *Purchasing and receiving*
   At least one month prior to the event, the
   equipment is rented, labor is contracted, and food
   is ordered and stored.
2. *Preparation time*
   Food preparation starts at least one day before the
   event. You need time to receive the fresh produce
   and meat. The food must be prepared and packed
   for transport.
3. *Travel time*
   On the day of the event, there must be time
   budgeted to load the food into the transports and
   travel to the location. Then you have to unload the
   food from the transports.
4. *Banquet setup time*
   The room(s) need to be cleaned and set up with
   tables, chairs, and buffet. Tables are draped and
   place settings, centerpieces, and printed materials
   are set up. Bars are also set up.
5. *Food preparation*
   The kitchen is set up, and last minute items are
   fetched—ice and baked goods. Food is reheated
   and arranged on trays and chafing dishes, or
   prepared for plating.

6. *Serving time*
   The actual time the food is to be served, from hors d'oeuvres to the dessert and coffee service. During this time the customary ceremonies will take place for each function, led by the master of ceremonies or the headwaiter.
7. *Kitchen cleanup time*
   All of the dishes and equipment must be washed and packed for transport. The appliances and floors of the kitchen facility need to be cleaned.
8. *Banquet cleanup time*
   The staff removes the dishes, linen, and equipment from the banquet room. The table and buffet setup are broken down. The premises are inspected by the banquet manager before the employees leave.
9. *Return travel time*
   The transports must be loaded and returned to the catering kitchen. Then the transports are unloaded, final washing is done, and everything put away so the kitchen is ready to be used again.

2 | *Sales*

For your catering business to be successful, you need a steady flow of clients. Repeat customers are vital, because they not only use your services, but they recommend you to others.

The salesperson is usually the only one who deals with the clients until the actual function takes place. The salesperson must know your business thoroughly, and be willing to work well with potential clients. The salesperson is your business representative, and has a big responsibility as far as public relations and promotion are concerned.

It's best to prepare a complete telephone pitch for people who call to inquire about your business. Your aim is to intrigue the client with the possibilities. Never rattle off a cut-and-dried answer of a price per head for each type of function. Instead, set up a date to meet with the client at the location in order to discuss the options.

Booking Dates

Before you go any further, make sure your business is available on the date and time the client requests. You should record all your catering functions in a reservation book for quick access.

If another function is already booked, be ready to offer alternative dates and times, pointing out there may be a price reduction for off-peak hours.

If the date is open, make a notation of the "tentative" function in the reservation book, and immediately book a date for the salesperson or banquet manager to view the location. (Of course, if the location is known, the salesperson can go immediately to the discussion of the specifications.)

The salesperson can help determine how to better serve your potential clientele by keeping track of such factors as:

What ages and income brackets are your clients?
Where do they live, and what are their occupations?
What sorts of functions are predominately booked?
Which functions do clients ask for most frequently?
Which days, dates, and times are most popular?
What do other caterers offer that attracts clients away from your business?

Client Specifications

In order to outline the catering options, you must first find out:

What type of function is the client planning?
How many guests are estimated?
When is the preferred date and time?
Where will the function be held?

The salesperson needs to listen to the practical aspects of what the client has in mind for their function. For example, a client may call and say she wants to throw an anniversary dinner for her parents for seventy-five people at the local country club. It's up to the salesperson to find out if a function of this size can take place at the country club, and to arrange for the location visit.

Other than the reason for the function and number of guests, the rest of the specifications should be left open until the location is visited. The salesperson can then give the potential client printed menus and brochures offering a variety of service styles, food, equipment, and outside services for their function. That leaves you the option of offering everything from an afternoon anniversary party package with cocktails and a string quartet, to a sit-down dinner with a band and dancing far into the night.

Make sure you also find out any special likes and dislikes a client may have. For example:

dietary requirements (low salt, low carbohydrate, low fat, vegetarian, kosher);
any special physical requirements (wheelchair access, or walker space);
any problems the client has encountered with past caterers or functions.

Package Plans

Package plans are created according to the types of functions your business caters. These basic plans can include the cost of food, beverages, labor, and outside services, broken down into a per-person price. You can also offer a list of options for your basic plans.

You'll need to scout around and find out what basic catering packages are selling for in your area. Determine the competitors' price ranges, the promotions they use, and what clients say as far as their service and food quality is concerned.

You may find it's better to add the price of outside services as extras, provided at additional flat rates. This drops the price per head of your basic package plans, and has a certain flexibility that may appeal to your clients.

Limiting the liquor is another good way to offer price reductions, but extras such as a glass of champagne or liqueur with dessert can be a nice option to offer your clients. You can print several package plans for each type of function, according to the budget level of your clients.

The salesperson should also promote your special offers and complimentary gifts, such as: free seconds on the dinner entrée, a glass of wine for each guest with dinner, valet parking, or coat-check and restroom attendants.

Estimates

Since each affair will have different requirements based on the location and specifications, prices at this point should be left approximate. Some caterers prefer to quote an approximate per-person charge based on their experience with similar functions. Others find it easier to accurately estimate costs by breaking down each function into categories: prices for food and beverages, labor, equipment, and additional costs (including overhead, payroll taxes, transportation, and employee meals).

Prices will vary depending on the time and day of the event, and whether the service is formal or informal. The price reduction of an afternoon wedding can help you book customers during the off-hours. You can also offer price reductions for large numbers of guests, for example: $24 per person for 100 guests, $23 per person for 150 guests, $22 per person for 200 guests, etc.

The client should be given only an approximate quote until one month before the function, when the details of the contract are settled and signed. This includes finalizing the guaranteed number of guests. However, you can tentatively book the client's function at the specified number of guests and estimated price per head on the date you agree to. A deposit can be made to hold the date until the contract is signed at which time the date is finalized.

The salesperson should follow up on tentative bookings, to find out if there are any adjustments you can make in

your offer that will better suit the client's needs and budget.
If you can find out why people decide not to book their
functions with you, then you can determine what you need
to offer in order to get clients.

Follow-up

The salesperson should get a report on each function from
the banquet manager regarding possible problems and/or
things that went off better than expected.

Then the salesperson should contact the client to find out
if everything went according to plan and without any
hitches. This is the perfect time to start selling the next
function.

3 | *Promotion and Advertising*

It's the little extra touches that make all the difference with clients who are shopping around for a caterer. It helps if you can offer unique food or drinks (serving daiquiris and margueritas from the bar), or if you dress your service staff in costumes to complement the occasion (clowns for kids' parties, western wear for barbecues, etc.).

Try to make each function different from any other. Often the best way to come up with something unique that suits the occasion is by talking to your client. Find out what's important in their life—family, hobbies, career. You may find out that the anniversary couple are both of Scottish descent, so you might accent the tables with their clan plaids. Or at a fund-raiser for a children's hospital, you can decorate the centerpieces with little dolls and toy cars.

Other decorative ideas are:

- Renting special uniforms for your service personnel in order to complement the client's color scheme
- Folding the napkins into fancy shapes like flowers, or birds
- Heating towels which are presented to each guest (with silver tongs from a silver tray) after the entrée
- Laying a single flower at the place of each female guest

- Printing special place cards
- Having party favors: miniature liquor bottles, flags, noisemakers, paper pumpkins, etc.
- Decorating cakes with real flowers

This doesn't mean piling on the extras—only a few special items should be showcased at each function, particularly when you're doing something big like ice sculptures, special lighting, or fountains.

Promotional Materials

To advertise your business and describe the various services you offer, you'll need promotional materials. Color brochures, letters, and complimentary reviews can help make your business more appealing to your clients.

You must create a professional brochure that features your package plans for the different functions. You also should emphasize in the brochure:

1. Your business changes menus regularly to better serve the needs of clients.
2. You buy the best quality food and merchandise to serve the guests.
3. Your service personnel are trained to perform their necessary duties with unobtrusive grace.
4. All your equipment, serviceware, and facilities are impeccably clean and of the highest quality.

Since menus do change regularly depending on market prices, sample menus should be printed on separate cards. It's also nice to have a linen chart of the various tablecloth and napkin colors, and samples of the flatware, china, and serviceware you offer.

For outside services, you'll need promotional material on floral arrangements, limousine services, musicians, entertainment, and photographers. When you're dealing with photographers, make sure to get prints of some of your functions and the way various meals look when they're served. Photographs of wedding and birthday cakes, Viennese tables, pastry carts, and a meat carving station with attendant chef are usually good images for advertising your business.

Food

Offer special food as a great way to make your catering business stand out from all the rest. Some nice ideas are:

- Ice cream with sauces
- Skewered meat and vegetables
- Carved vegetables: radish, tomato, and turnip roses
- Crosshatch potato fries
- Silver bowls or cornucopias of fruit
- Baskets made of glazed bread
- Melon bowls for melon balls
- Scalloped shells for shrimp salad
- Butter molds in individual serving shapes

You can also spice up traditional dishes in unique ways. Garnish soup with a cucumber slice on cream of cucumber; shredded beets or a dollop of sour cream on top of borscht. Or serve unusual breads such as croissants, popovers, baguettes, or whole loaves of bread sliced by one of your service personnel. You can also individually box up dessert leftovers for guests to take home.

With drinks, you can garnish them with vegetable sticks, or fruit on sticks (strawberries, melon balls, orange and pineapple chunks, and cherries). Or float fruit in punch bowls, and lemon slices in water glasses and pitchers.

Whenever you agree to special cooking preparations—a chef preparing cherries jubilee, or the waiters tossing a caesar salad for each table—first make sure your service personnel can handle it.

Gifts

When a client has given your business thousands of dollars to produce their special event, it's nice to give them something tangible to hold onto after the function is over. A unique way to celebrate each function is to place one of the invitations in a silver frame and present it to the hosts at the end of the night as a keepsake.

With wedding receptions, you can give the cake knife to the couple, engraved with best wishes from your business. Or you can give special champagne glasses to the bridal or anniversary couple.

Promotional giveaways can also be provided for each guest, printed with your business name and logo: matchbooks, stirrers, key chains, etc.

Advertising

Word of mouth is the best advertising a catering business can get. You want all of your clients to be completely satisfied by their functions, and this means acceding to outrageous whims both before and during the function.

If a function has the potential for breaking you into a new circle of people, or introducing your business to a popular banquet hall, then by all means cut into your profit margin if you have to. The payoff in future business will be well worth it.

When you list your business in the Yellow Pages, consider having it printed in bold type, or boxed to highlight the name. You can list it under caterers, party planners, or meeting planners.

Advertising in local newspapers or magazines should be targeted to particular groups: ethnic, social, age, income-bracket, or for specific functions. For example, you can advertise in bridal magazines to draw requests only for wedding receptions.

Direct Mail

You can mail letters and brochures directly to potential clients to promote your business and services.

Contact fund-raising groups, charities, and political organizations, and ask if you can quote a price for their next function. Even social groups like the Kiwanis club or church groups hold a party at least once a year.

You can contact local businesses in the area to solicit seminar and meeting business. And you can contact potential clients according to their professional groups through organizations and trade journals.

Schools almost always have annual reunions, proms, and homecoming events, and they offer a wealth of potential graduation parties. And you can contact recreational facilities, such as bowling alleys, water-sports arenas, and skating or roller rinks to find out how you can offer package deals for children's and teen parties.

If weddings are your specialty, then focus on engagement announcements in your local paper. A note of congratulations to the happy brides-to-be, along with a tasteful display of your package options, can generate plenty of business for you.

4 | *Planning Menus*

Create standard menus for each type of meal, particularly the ones that are high demand in your area. You may find that you serve more luncheons than dinners, or more cocktail parties than wedding receptions.

For each type of meal, you can offer an additional list of special items, or create several menus for each type of function. This enables you to duplicate ingredients for various food items, which helps when it comes to purchasing and preparing the meals.

Menus are planned taking into account the number of guests attending, the timing of the event, the type of service provided, and the price per person.

It's up to the salesperson to recommend menu options that suit the specifications and budget of the client, while returning a reasonable profit for your business. This ensures that each function will be a high-quality event.

Every guest at the event is a potential customer, so menus should never be negotiated for lower quality in return for lower cost. By consistently creating balanced affairs at various price levels, you will steadily gain more clients.

There are a few things you should keep in mind while you are planning your menus:

1. Each food item has to be prepared in a way that is visually pleasing, complementing the other foods served.

2. In general, you should avoid spicy or unusual
   food, unless the client specifically requests it.
   Even then, you may want to recommend something that would be more universally liked by
   their guests.
3. Be sure to incorporate local food or preparation
   preferences when planning your menus.

Print your menus in elegant type, with clear, easy-to-read
descriptions. Food items should be listed in the order they
will be served.

Buffet

A buffet is any meal served from a large table, with the food
attractively displayed. Buffets create a relaxed, informal
atmosphere and a wider variety of food can be offered to the
guests.

The banquet tables should be set up with the silverware,
glassware, napkins, and condiments already in place. You
can distribute small trays of appetizers on each table at the
beginning of the meal. This gives the guests something to
nibble on, controlling the flow to the buffet. Or you can have
the headwaiter (or master of ceremonies) invite one table at a
time to the buffet, beginning with the hosts' table.

Though buffets are more informal than sit-down dinners,
they aren't necessarily less expensive. You must provide
more food per guest since they often return to the buffet
several times. And the preparation for the large selection of
food can take more time than a pre-plated meal. You need
the same number of service people per guests as at sit-down
dinners, and you have the added expense of setting up the
buffet table (linen, skirting, chafing dishes, decoration, and
fine serviceware).

Buffet Setup

A typical buffet will offer a variety of appetizers, entrées, cold meats, salads, vegetables, assorted rolls, cheese platters, fresh fruit, and desserts.

Consider the layout carefully to make sure the display is appealing to the eye. Use complementary colors, volumes, and shapes of dishes in order to enhance the food presentation. Floral arrangements shouldn't detract from the food, but you can use cut flowers and table ferns to surround each dish or tray. If you can, use fine crystal and silver serviceware.

Always serve food from cold to hot so that the hot items stay hotter longer. The proper sequence for a buffet is:

1. China
2. Cold food—salads, cold platters, cheese, breads
3. Hot food—potatoes, vegetables, meat, and fish

A hot carving station can be added to the buffet for an additional fee. You need to hire a properly uniformed chef for a professional appearance to carve the meat (roast beef, brisket of beef, roast turkey, hot corned beef, pastrami, etc.). Equipment includes a cutting board with drain and clamped heat lamps to display the carved meat.

A separate table beyond the carving station should hold assorted desserts and fresh fruits. Desserts can also be served from a tableside rolling cart.

Service

Once the guests have been seated at their tables, they come forward to the buffet to select from the display of hot and cold foods. You'll have a good service flow if you set up one buffet for every fifty to seventy-five guests.

Your service personnel are assigned to three positions:

1. Servers—a group to serve behind the buffet table(s)

2. Waiters—a group to serve beverages and clear dishes from tables
3. Runners—one or two people (depending on the number of guests) to replenish the buffet table when items are low

The servers should serve the food from the buffet rather than letting the guests help themselves—it creates a much more polished effect. It also helps control the amount of food that is distributed.

The line of guests flows along one side of the table, with the servers positioned on the other, explaining the various food items and their respective ingredients. They should also unobtrusively maintain the appearance of the food and table.

The runners inform the kitchen about depleted items on the buffet table. Dishes that are two-thirds empty should be replaced with a fresh one that is full. Clean linen should be used as potholders on hot dishes. The leftover food is returned to the cook, and the soiled tray is given to dishwashers.

Sit-down Dinner

Sit-down dinners are the most common type of meal for evening affairs. They are generally preferred for formal occasions, and there is usually dancing after the meal.

Each course is pre-plated in the kitchen and served by the waiters. Dinner can include: a cold appetizer, bread, soup, salad, intermezzo (sherbet or crème de menthe to cleanse the palate), entrée (meat, potato, vegetable), and dessert. Courses can be added or eliminated depending on the budget of the client.

Beverages usually include coffee, tea, milk, soda, and juice. Wine is also very popular with dinner, as well as beer.

Gourmet dinners are special, multicourse meals that are

intended to create an elaborate dining experience. These are high-cost affairs, requiring elaborate food preparation, impeccable service and serviceware, and fine wines and after-dinner cordials.

Cocktail Party

Cocktail parties are very popular because they can accommodate large numbers of guests at relatively low prices. The setting is informal, giving you wide latitude in the special options you can offer. The fee is usually charged on an hourly basis, depending on the specifications.

Cocktail parties can either be arranged as separate affairs or they can be held prior to a dinner function. Late afternoon and early evening are the proper times for a cocktail party, though some clients will request a cocktail hour prior to a luncheon event (for retirement functions or bachelor parties).

A combination of food and liquor is usually provided by the caterer. Clients may prefer to have liquor served only during the cocktail hour (due to cost or personal preference). If the liquor sale is projected to be high enough, you can offer a selection of hot and/or cold appetizers to be served gratis.

Service

Only hors d'oeuvres that are easy to handle should be served. Food that is messy, greasy, or with bones or shells shouldn't be offered to the client. Remember that most of the guests will remain standing during the cocktail hour, with one hand holding a drink.

There are two different types of service for cocktail parties—butler style and buffet.

Butler style is the service of assorted hot hors d'oeuvres and cold canapés, offered to each guest on a silver tray.

These should be finger foods, arranged on doilies or speared by toothpick frills, and accompanied by a paper cocktail napkin.

Butler style is the most elegant arrangement, and offers the added advantage of being the cheapest. You can sell hors d'oeuvres by the piece or by the tray (designating how many hors d'oeuvres on a tray). The average consumption rate is six to eight hors d'oeuvres per customer per hour.

With buffet service, more food needs to be offered, including hot chafing dish items, cold platters, salads (be careful of messiness), cheeses, and fruit arrangements. Small-size plates, silverware, and napkins are usually provided, and enough tables to give adequate seating for the guests.

Luncheon

Luncheons can be anything from a formal sit-down for a ladies' charity group, to a lunch buffet set up between business meetings and seminars.

The luncheon menu is less elaborate than for dinner: either soup or a cold appetizer; entrée, with potato and vegetable; dessert; and coffee.

Take into account the type of guests who will attend when you plan the food and liquor. A bridal luncheon should consist of lighter fare, with champagne or a punch bowl, while a business luncheon relies on lots of coffee and hot, generous portions.

Breakfast

Don't overlook morning functions as a source of jobs. Most businesses favor breakfast meetings, which are easy to produce and execute.

The key to a successful breakfast is to serve plenty of good coffee from the moment the first guest takes his seat.

Then keep on serving coffee throughout the event. You'll serve more coffee at breakfast than at any other meal.

Once the guests are seated, immediately place items such as juice, pastries, rolls, bagels, butter, cream cheese, and jam on the tables. This gives the guests something to munch on with their coffee while they're waiting for service.

The other key to a successful breakfast is planning the preparation and/or transport so that the food is served hot and fast. Depending on the size of the group, the food can either be pre-plated in the kitchen or served on platters.

It's a nice touch to provide chafing dishes on a side table for guests who want seconds (otherwise you'll get complaints of insufficient food). Obviously, buffet-style breakfasts are best when you plan to offer a selection of food items.

Brunch

The function is referred to as a brunch when the meal falls between late morning and early afternoon, and includes a combination of breakfast and luncheon foods.

The most popular brunch items include: eggs (prepared in various ways), quiches, crepes, pancakes, waffles, French toast, ham, bacon, sausage, steak, herring, lox, fresh fruit, fried potatoes, toast, bagels, rolls, Danish, and muffins. You should offer a variety of teas, plenty of good coffee, milk, and fruit juices.

Since variety seems to be the key for a successful brunch, it's best to offer the food buffet-style. But if you want a more formal event, brunch items can be served on platters at the tables.

For a truly elaborate brunch—such as a champagne wedding brunch—a chef can prepare items like omelettes and crepes right in front of the guests. He should be dressed in a white uniform, and stand on a platform with portable burners. Waiters then serve the hot fillings for the crepes from chafing dishes.

Coffee Break

These are usually provided at meetings, promotional events, and other group functions. Light foods and beverages are offered, such as cookies, Danish, and pastries, with plenty of coffee, assorted teas, fruit juices, and milk.

Box Lunch

These are portable lunches or dinners used for meetings, picnics, sporting events, and informal gatherings. The meal itself can be simple or quite elaborate, depending on the budget of the client.

You can offer two sets of boxed lunches, so the guests have an option, but then you'll have to provide extra, assuming that it won't work out exactly right.

Offer two different sandwiches in each box, along with a few of the following items: vegetable sticks and flowers, potato salad, coleslaw, fruit, cheese, bread or crackers, and a dessert such as cookies, pastry, or individual cakes.

Each lunch should include a napkin, salt, pepper, spoon, fork, and knife.

5 | *Menus for Different Functions*

You can offer various food and service options for each type of function, depending on the location, number of guests, and budget. The following is a description of the most common functions that your business can cater, along with sample menus.

Anniversary Party

This is a celebratory event later in a couple's life, so the party is often quite lavish. The function can take the form of a luncheon, dinner, or buffet with either formal or informal service.

The silver (25th) and golden (50th) anniversaries are the most celebrated. Try to incorporate the symbolic material of each anniversary into your decorations: 1st (paper), 5th (wood), 10th (tin), 15th (crystal), 20th (china), and 35th (coral).

The guests of honor are usually seated at a decorated dais table, or in the center of a long table. As with wedding receptions, the headwaiter or master of ceremonies conducts a formal introduction of the anniversary couple, announces the first dance, and supervises the cake-cutting ceremony.

Liquor is usually served during the cocktail hour, during the meal, and/or after dinner. Champagne and other liquor arrangements can be sold separately or incorporated into the package plan for an anniversary party.

An anniversary cake is usually substituted as a dessert course. Cakes can be either tiered and topped with an ornament, or a single layer (sheet cake) with an appropriate inscription.

• Fancy Buffet Menu
(30–120 guests)

There will be a selection of hot hors d'oeuvres, cold canapés, and cold sliced meat and cheese platters with assorted bread and rolls.

Appetizers	Shrimp cocktail
	Liver pâté
Entrées	Beef Stroganoff, with buttered noodles
	Curry chicken, with wild rice
	Coq au vin, with potatoes
Sides	Vegetable casserole
	Cheese blintzes with sour cream
	Caesar salad
	Fruit tray
Dessert	Lemon iced cake, with sherbet

• Dinner Menu
(20–60 guests)

A glass of wine will be served with the meal, and beverages throughout.

Appetizer	Tomato and mozzarella cheese slices
	Tossed green salad
Dinner	1. Baked salmon steak with wine sauce
(choose one)	Browned potato
	Fresh garden peas

2. Eggplant parmesan
   Baked ziti
   Green beans and walnuts
3. Roast half chicken with basil
   Parsley potato slices
   Sweet corn
4. Chicken-mushroom souffle
   Baked potato
   Fresh garden peas

Dessert   French pastries, or
                   Ice cream

• Menu Alternatives

Alternative food choices can be listed separately, either
on the menus themselves or on a separate listing by
category:

Entrées   Chow mein, with crispy noodles
                   Sweet and sour chicken, with fried rice
                   Roast beef, with Yorkshire pudding
                   Fish and chips
                   Knockwurst, with sauerkraut
                   Stuffed cabbage
                   Barbecued spare ribs
                   Beef Stroganoff
                   Beef lasagna

Vegetables   Baked yellow squash
                   Antipasto
                   Vinaigrette salad
                   Leek salad

Desserts   Crepes suzette, from a chafing dish
                   Almond cookies
                   Pound cake
                   Fruit compote

Engagement Parties and Bridal Showers

These functions can be arranged as a cocktail party, breakfast, luncheon, sit-down dinner, or buffet supper. Champagne, liquor, and/or punch bowls are usually offered to the guests.

Guests usually bring gifts, so a gift table should be provided near the host's table. Showers include a gift-opening ceremony, and an appropriately decorated cake. Engagement parties also include dancing, and an engagement cake with a cutting ceremony by the couple.

Though these events are usually small, you should take special care to create a memorable function. Think of it as an auditioning for the job of catering the wedding reception.

• Formal Breakfast Menu
(15–30 guests)

Coffee, tea, assorted fruit juices, milk, and champagne served throughout.

Appetizer	Cheese and blueberry blintzes
	Fresh fruit
Entrée	French toast wedges, or
	Dutch *panekokes*, or
	Waffles with fruit, or
	Minced ham omelet
	Sausages and bacon
	Toast (wheat, white, rye)
	Assorted Danish
	English muffins
	Jam, marmalade, butter

Rehearsal Dinner

A rehearsal dinner is given for the entire bridal party after they rehearse the wedding ceremony.

It is usually paid for by the groom's parents, since traditionally most of the other expenses of the wedding are paid for by the bride's parents. This can be the groom's mother's time to shine, and she may want to include special arrangements such as flowers, music, formal service, and champagne.

- **Formal Dinner Menu**
  (10–25 guests)

  Cocktail hour from 7:00 A.M. to 8:00 P.M., with assorted hot hors d'oeuvres and cold canapés served butler style.

Appetizer	Tomato aspic
	Shellfish salad
Soup	Cream of cucumber, or
	French onion
Entrée	Veal scallopini,
	Chateaubriand, or
	Cornish hen
	Noodles Alfredo
	Tossed salad
	Dinner rolls, with butter
Dessert	Cherries jubilee, or
	Chocolate soufflé

Retirement Dinner

Retirement dinners are usually sponsored by an employer or business organization to honor a retiring employee. The guest of honor should be seated at the head of the table, or in the center of the dais table. If speeches and awards are to be given, a lectern with a microphone should be placed in the center of the dais, next to the guest of honor.

Retirement dinners are considered happy events,

celebrating a lifetime of achievement. A cocktail hour is usually included, whether the event is a luncheon or dinner. At the very least, a cash bar should be offered to the guests.

Often a cake is ordered with an inscription of farewell and good luck.

• Luncheon Menu
(25–125 guests)

Cocktails served one hour prior to luncheon, either open bar or cash bar.

Appetizer	Fruit cup, with whipped cream, or Shrimp cocktail
Entrée	Shrimp Louis, with fruit and cheese Chicken à la king, with toast, or Turkey tetrazzini
	Green vegetable, or Sweet creamed corn Rolls, biscuits, with butter
Dessert	Individual fruit tarts

• Dinner Menu
(25–125 guests)

Cocktails served one hour prior to the dinner service, either open bar or cash bar. A glass of wine is served with the meal, along with coffee, soda, and juice.

Appetizer	Fruit cup (fresh fruit in season), or Vichyssoise
Entrée	Prime ribs of beef au jus, or Filet of sole Florentine
	Browned potatoes Tomato slices on bed of lettuce Dinner rolls, with butter

Dessert   Assorted French pastries (four per person)

Birthday Party

Birthday parties can be held at any time of day, and can be a breakfast, brunch, luncheon, or dinner. Usually the food service is buffet-style, creating an informal, relaxed affair.

The caterer should always provide a gift table for the birthday presents. The headwaiter should arrange the cake-cutting ceremony after the coffee has been served.

Children's birthday parties should take the child's preferences into consideration during the planning stages. Sweet Sixteen parties are usually for girls, but many don't like the idea of pink and white decorations. Instead, hold teen parties in a popular amusement site, and serve food such as pizza, fried chicken, hamburgers, frankfurters, and french fries. Contemporary music can also be provided for dancing.

One of the most popular ways to throw a party for a large group (birthday, graduation, bon voyage parties) is a cocktail reception. It starts anywhere from 4:00 P.M. to 7:00 P.M. and can last from one to three or more hours.

• Cocktail Reception Menu
(40–150 guests)

A glass of champagne is served to all the guests. The open bar serves throughout the party.

Assorted decorated canapés and hot hors d'oeuvres
Assorted finger sandwiches (avocado, cucumber, cream cheese, eggplant)
Assorted French pastries
Birthday cake

Coffee, tea, soda, juice

• **Children's Birthday Lunch Menu**
  (under twelve years of age)

  Punch, soda, chilled fruit juice, milk and chocolate milk will be served throughout

Appetizers	Miniature hamburgers
	Miniature hot dogs
Entrée	Chicken salad sandwich, or
	Grilled cheese sandwich, with tomato, or
	Chicken fingers
	Curly fries
Salad	Fruit salad
(choose one)	Macaroni salad
	Potato salad
Dessert	Birthday cake and ice cream

• **Teen's Birthday Dinner Menu**

  Soda, chilled fruit juice, and punch will be served throughout.

Appetizers	Cheese pastry puffs
	Fruit cup
Entrée	Fried chicken fingers, with sauce (barbecue, honey mustard, sweet and sour), or
	Turkey sandwich supreme
	Curly fries
Salad	Fruit salad
(choose two)	Macaroni salad
	Potato salad
	Coleslaw
Dessert	Birthday cake and ice cream

Theme Parties

Theme parties can be held by businesses, individuals, and social, religious, and organizational groups, either for profit or purely for enjoyment. Usually there is dancing or some sort of event like an auction, fashion show, or special entertainment.

From square dances and costume parties to ethnic celebrations and reunion dinners, theme parties are arranged around one unifying event. Holiday celebrations include: Christmas, Easter, Valentine's Day, St. Patrick's Day, and Halloween. Surprise parties can also be considered theme parties, because they require special care in arranging so as not to spoil the surprise.

Since these parties are fun social affairs, a festive spirit should prevail. A cash bar, where drinks are sold individually to guests, usually works best. Light food can also be offered buffet-style, or as sit-down service.

The food and decorations incorporate the theme of the party: you can offer entire package plans of food, decorations, music, and entertainment to help ensure a successful affair.

• Barbecue Dinner Menu
(10–50 guests)

All meat will be cooked in full view of guests, on outdoor grills, open pits, or barbecues. Either sit-down service or buffet-style.

Meat	New York steak
(choice of two,	Kabobs (beef, lamb, or chicken with
and sauce)	vegetables)
	Fresh fish filets (seasonal)
	Turkey
	Ham steaks
	Rack of lamb

(choose one)   Fresh broiled corn on the cob
Idaho potato (baked)
Sweet potato (baked)
Assorted relishes
Coleslaw
Tossed green salad
Hot biscuits, with butter

Dessert   Pie (apple, Boston cream, pecan)

Beverages   Coffee, tea, soda, beer

Fund-raising Functions

These functions are organized by a variety of political, religious, and business associations, as well as charities, foundations, unions, and non-profit organizations.

Since tickets are sold prior to the event, you must get a guarantee on the final head count. Ask your client to report any anticipated percentage over or under the number of guaranteed guests according to the sale of the tickets. This way, you can adjust your purchasing in order to avoid disagreements on final charges.

Fund-raisers usually include a printed program, which sells ads to local businesses. Buy or barter for advertising space in the program—potential clients will remember the name of your business much more easily if they've seen it advertised. And you can usually write off the cost as a charitable contribution.

• Fancy Breakfast Menu
(25–150 guests)

A glass of champagne or mimosa served to each guest. Chilled fruit juice, coffee, assorted teas, and milk served throughout.

Appetizer   Assorted cheese platters, or
Smoked fish platters

Entrée   Cream cheese omelet,
              Pancakes, or
              Waffles
              Sausage or bacon
              English muffins
              Hot biscuits
              Sweet rolls

• **Fancy Dinner Menu**
  (30–100 guests)

  Cocktail hour from 5:00 P.M. to 6:00 P.M. with assorted
  hot and cold hors d'oeuvres passed butler style.

Appetizer   Shrimp cocktail, or
              Quiche lorraine
Entrée   Roast beef au jus
              Sirloin steak
              London broil, or
              Ham steak

              Foil-wrapped baked potato
              Garden peas with almond slices
              Dinner roll, with butter
Dessert   Individual strawberry shortcake

Promotional Shows

Promotional shows are usually held to highlight exhibits or
displays. Trade functions fall into this category, as well as
PR events and some types of business gatherings (like
stockholders' meetings). You can get great exposure among
professional clients by catering these types of events.

Conventions and trade shows can include everything
from gem shows to antique boutiques, fashion displays to
flower shows. This type of function requires a great deal of
cooperation between the management of the space and the

organizers of the show. The caterer must be clear who she is responsible to throughout the event.

- **Basic Dinner Menu**
  (25–150 guests)

  No cocktail hour. For functions over fifty, cash bar available.

Appetizer	Fresh garden salad
Entrée	New York cut steak, or Salisbury steak
	Baked potato, with sour cream and chives
	Spring baby peas
	Dinner roll, with butter
Dessert	Choice of chocolate or vanilla mousse
Beverages	Coffee, tea, soda

Meetings and Seminars

With meetings and seminars, the primary goal is to convey information. These gatherings of selected groups also provide opportunities for networking, incentive boosting, and creating a sense of comradery among business associates.

The meal times are consider break times, allowing the participants to relax and talk among themselves. It offers the humanizing balance that group instruction desperately needs.

While one set of rooms is used as a meeting area, other rooms are set up for dining. The schedule for the function depends on the demands and budget of the client.

A sample schedule of a convention for one hundred regional sales representatives could go as follows:

Room	Activity	Time
A	Continental Breakfast	8:00–9:00 A.M.
B	Meeting	9:00–10:30
A	Coffee Break	10:30–11:00
B	Meeting	11:00–12:30 P.M.
A	Lunch	12:30–1:30
B	Meeting	1:30–3:00
A	Coffee Break	3:00–3:30
B	Meeting	3:30–5:00
A	Cocktail Party	5:00–6:00
B	Dinner	6:00–7:30

• Coffee Break Menu
(10–150 guests)

Coffee, tea, or milk	$1 per person, or $10 per gallon (25 cups)
Soda	$2 per person
Fruit juice	$2 per person
Danish pastries	$3 per person
Assorted cookies	$1 per person

• Budget Luncheon Menu
(50–150 guests)

Coffee, tea, soda, and fruit juice served throughout.

Appetizer	Grilled cheese squares, or Cottage cheese and fruit cup
Entrée	Chicken mushroom sandwich, Hot turkey sandwich, or Tomato, cheese and cucumber sandwich
	Tossed green salad
Dessert	Cake slices

6 | *Wedding Receptions*

The most elaborate catered event is a wedding reception. A multibillion dollar industry is generated annually by weddings, and some people save for years in order to have their "dream" wedding.

This doesn't mean it's easy to make money catering wedding receptions. You must be willing and able to accommodate whims and sudden changes in every stage of the event. The caterer must also be familiar with all aspects of the wedding preparations for each client so the reception can be planned as an integral part of the wedding festivities.

It's not enough to find out whether the couple wants an informal or formal affair. You have to determine the right tone for the evening. Take hints from the client—are the bride and her mother making the arrangements? Or is it the bride and groom? Or even the bride alone? What sorts of guests are being invited—business associates? College friends? How many family members? You may discover that the bride is primarily inviting her Greek relatives, while the groom is inviting friends and associates from the film industry. This could be an interesting mix, if you exploit it with the right combination of ethnic food and music, presented with an upbeat, professional flair.

Saturdays and Sundays are the most popular days for weddings. Afternoon affairs (from noon to 5:00 P.M.) are sold at lower rates than evening affairs, which can go from 7:00 P.M. into the early morning hours. Overtime rates are usually applied after five hours. Brunches and informal weddings are often held in the morning or weekday afternoons.

May and June are traditionally the months for weddings, but September and October are also popular months. It's common to offer special rates for off-season months.

Wedding Rituals

The caterer should be conversant with the different rituals that take place during the wedding reception, from the bridal introduction to the cake-cutting ceremony. Either the master of ceremonies (band leader, wedding planner) or the headwaiter directs the rest of the wedding party in performing these ceremonies.

Before the day of the reception, the banquet manager should get from the bride a list of all the names of the wedding party. It's handy to have a form for filling out the participants' names. Then the headwaiter only needs to consult the list in order to announce the wedding party.

The bride has the final say on how the rituals of the wedding reception are carried out. The banquet manager should be sure to set the tone that the bride dictates.

Introduction of the Bridal Party

The introduction takes place after the cocktail hour, when the guests have been seated in the banquet room. The headwaiter should organize the sequence of the entry of the wedding party into the banquet room.

Then the wedding party enters in couples as the master of ceremonies or headwaiter introduces the wedding party. The bride's parents are first, then the groom's parents, followed by the bridesmaids and ushers, the maid of honor and best man. If there is a ring bearer or flower girl, they are introduced next.

Sometimes the couples separate as they enter, facing each other as they line up to form an aisle. In military weddings, swords and bouquets are raised to form an arch over the aisle. Then the bride and groom walk through the aisle to stand in front of the wedding cake as they are introduced for the first time as Mr. and Mrs.

First Dance

The master of ceremonies takes the bouquets to free the couples for the first dance (usually the bouquets are laid out around the cake or gift table to add a decorative touch).

The master of ceremonies then announces the couple's first dance as man and wife. They dance for a few minutes, the guests clap, then the master of ceremonies asks the rest of the wedding party to join them in dancing. The parents can either join after a few minutes, or choose to sit down.

The rest of the guests are then invited to join in the dancing. Usually the wedding party leaves the floor at this point in order to take their seats at the bridal table.

Bridal Table

The bridal table is the focus of the room. The bride and groom are seated in the center, with the maid of honor next to either the bride or the groom. From that point on, bridesmaids alternate with ushers in the usual man/woman seating.

Sometimes, the bridal couple is seated at a separate table in order to allow guests to freely come up and congratulate them. The rest of the wedding party and parents are seated at surrounding tables.

Toasts

The dancing continues until champagne has been served to the wedding party and the rest of the guests. Then the master of ceremonies invites the clergyman or other member to say grace (if it is a religious ceremony). Otherwise, the emcee calls on the best man to give the first toast.

During the first toast, all of the guests stand except for the bride and groom. The best man gives a short, prepared speech while holding his glass up to the bride and groom. If the best man is clueless, you can suggest he follow tradition and direct his toast toward complimenting the bride, concluding with best wishes for both of them.

Additional toasting may take place while the serving begins. No more ceremonies are conducted until the cake cutting. However, if the bride wishes, the emcee can announce a solo dance for the bride and her father following the dinner service.

Jewish Wedding Rituals

Jewish wedding receptions are slightly different in that the bride and groom enter the banquet room after everyone else is already seated, and they alone are introduced to the guests. Also, the parents of the bride are usually seated at the bridal table along with the wedding party.

After the couple is introduced, a short prayer (*moitze*) is recited over the challah bread. This prayer is usually said by the eldest person present, a grandparent or uncle.

After each person in the wedding party eats a piece of the challah, the remainder is taken to the kitchen where it is sliced into small chunks and placed on platters. Waiters go from table to table, offering the bread for the guests to eat.

The best man can either give his toast then, or once the dinner has begun.

Dinner

Since a wedding is a formal affair, it is usually a sit-down dinner. The menu is similar to that of a formal dinner, except that dessert is omitted since the wedding cake will be served.

It's best to offer half a dozen special menus to potential clients, and have a list of suggested alternatives. Even if the client goes for a choice of roast prime top sirloin or broiled Alaskan salmon, make sure an unusual or elegant side dish is added to give the meal something special.

The Wedding Cake

The wedding cake must be gorgeous. Because wedding cakes involve so much time and artistic effort, most caterers order them from outside bakers. The chef or food purchaser must ensure the cake is ordered to meet the client's specifications. It is usually picked up the day of the wedding reception.

Always go with superior quality when it comes to purchasing wedding cakes. It's the last food item the guests will eat, and even though it's not technically from your kitchen, it will strongly affect their opinion of the entire meal. Besides, the guests stare at the cake throughout the reception and their expectations are high. Don't disappoint them with the taste.

Price

The price markup is usually quite high for wedding cakes. If the bakery charges $.75 for a slice, caterers can charge up to $1.25. The bakery would like to charge $1.50 to a customer who came in off the street to order their cake, but caterers get a deal because of their repeat business.

If you can't accommodate your client at a reasonable price, then have a superior pastry chef you can recommend. It doesn't matter if the cost is slightly more, your recommendation should be for only the best.

Presentation

Presentation is a big part of the wedding cake—even if you don't make the cake, the headwaiter still has to arrange the cake table.

A separate, draped table should be positioned to best advantage in the room. If you can, harmonize the colors of the decoration with the bridal bouquets so that you can make the cake appear to float on a sea of flowers when they are laid on the table.

Wedding cakes can come in almost any shape: round, oval, diamond, heart-shaped, square, and rectangular. But the most typical, of course, is graduated, round tiers.

Some cakes incorporate fountains either between the tiers or at the base. All cakes are ornamented on the top tier, which is wrapped up as a keepsake. Your chef should be prepared to wrap this tier for long-term freezing, since many couples want to enjoy this cake on their first anniversary.

Cutting the Wedding Cake

The cutting ceremony takes place after the entrée has been served and eaten, while the coffee service is being prepared. If guests have begun dancing again, the headwaiter or master of ceremonies announces the cutting ceremony by calling the bride and groom to the cake.

The headwaiter shows the bride where to hold the knife, while the groom is instructed to place his right hand over hers. The photographer will want the couple to remain in this pose in order to get a few good shots. The photographer will often direct the actual slicing of the first piece from the bottom tier, as well as the cake-feeding, with the bride serving the groom first.

The headwaiter should be ready with a napkin to hand to the bride, and another for the groom. He unobtrusively hands the used plate and uneaten portions to the bridal waiter, who places them at the bride and groom's seats at the bridal table.

The cake is either removed to the kitchen or cut in front of the guests. If a great deal of dismantling needs to take place (removing tiers and ornaments), then roll the entire cake table into the kitchen so the guests don't have to see it being destroyed.

Serving the Cake

The headwaiter will need a glass of hot water in which to dip the knife to make the cutting easier. Each tier is sliced into concentric rings about two inches thick. Then vertical slices are made around the rim, creating two-inch wedges.

The bridal table is served first, followed by the bride's parents, then the rest of the guests. Coffee and tea should flow freely at this time—and champagne, as well, if the budget permits.

Sometimes a large cake is cut into smaller portions which are gift-wrapped for the guests. These are placed on a draped table near the exit, and can be distributed by one of the waiters as the guests leave.

If the client supplies their own wedding cake, most caterers charge a cake-cutting and clean-up fee of about 25¢ a slice. Make sure your clients understand this will be part of the total bill for your services.

Throwing the Bridal Bouquet

The bride usually throws the bouquet just prior to her departure. If the couple plans to stay, the throwing cere-mony is the signal of the end of the official reception, so the couple can change into more comfortable evening clothes to finish the rest of the party.

The master of ceremonies announces the throwing of the bridal bouquet by summoning all unmarried women to the dance floor. The bride stands only a few feet away, with her back to the rest. She tosses the bouquet up into the air and slightly behind her, so it comes down directly over the top of the group of girls.

It helps if there is an elevated place where the bride can stand—either the band platform or a flight of stairs. It also makes a pretty photograph, with the bride elevated above her friends.

The master of ceremonies should announce the name of the woman who catches the bouquet and her relationship to the bride and groom, adding that legend says she will be the next to marry.

Throwing the Garter

It's up to the bride to decide if her garter will be thrown by the groom. She is seated on a chair that is brought to the center of the floor by the headwaiter. Then the groom kneels and removes the garter from her thigh.

He goes through the same tossing ceremony with the eligible bachelors, throwing the garter high into the air over their heads.

The man who catches it receives the privilege of placing it on the thigh of the single lady who caught the bouquet (if she agrees). This lady is seated on the same chair the bride used, as the man kneels in front of her. Under the direction of the master of ceremonies, he places the garter on her thigh.

After this, if the bride and groom wish to change, the headwaiter should direct them to the dressing rooms that have been set aside for their use. They either return to the reception, or make last-minute farewells to the guests, and depart together. Caterers sometimes help arrange the first night's lodging at a nearby hotel or bed & breakfast.

The cost of the wedding and reception are usually assumed by the bride and her family. However, sometimes it is the bride and groom who pay, or the groom's parents or other relatives who are involved in the financing. Sometimes family members choose to pay for specific parts of the wedding reception—such as the band, or the flowers, or the liquor, or the cake. This should be decided prior to the function, and the headwaiter should be prepared to supply separate billing for each party at the conclusion of the function.

• Wedding Dinner Menu
(50–150 guests)

Cocktails served one hour prior to dinner service. A glass of champagne with fresh strawberry served to each guest. A glass of white wine served with dinner. Open bar following coffee service.

Appetizers (served buffet style):	Cold sliced meat trays (ham and cheese, turkey, salami, tongue, picnic meats) Sliced cheese trays hot hors d'oeuvres cold canapes
Salad	Shrimp salad Cottage cheese and cherry tomatoes
Entrée	Rigatoni, with vodka sauce, Lemon chicken with mashed potatoes, or Swedish meatballs, with mushrooms Wild rice pilaf Fresh green vegetables

Desserts   Assorted cookies
                            wedding cake
Beverage   Coffee, tea, milk, soda

• Breakfast Wedding Menu
  (25–150 guests)

Champagne cocktails served first. Breakfast is served at
11:00 A.M.

Entrée   Mushroom omelet with cream
                            cheese, or
                            Eggs Benedict with hollandaise
                            sauce

                            Fruit cup with melon balls
                            Assorted Danish
                            English muffins
Dessert   Traditional wedding cake

7 | *Bar Mitzvah*

Aside from wedding receptions, the most profitable function you can cater is a bar mitzvah. These are usually large, formal occasions with large amounts of food and liquor served to the guests.

The bar mitzvah ceremony is one of the most important holy days in Jewish life, and is held in the synagogue on the Sabbath prior to the boy's thirteenth birthday. Many people also hold bat mitzvahs for their daughters.

The caterer could be asked to provide a light refreshment at the synagogue after the ceremony, so that family and friends can celebrate the occasion. This is known as a *kiddush*, and consists of: cold platters, pastries, sponge cake, honey cake, pound cake, strudel, *rugalah*, wine, and beverages. Only kosher food and equipment can be brought to synagogues.

Cocktail Reception

When setting up an elaborate bar mitzvah, make sure to offer plenty of food right away. Hors d'oeuvres should be passed in the cocktail area as the guests arrive, or the buffet should be ready to serve. The buffet consists of hot and cold appetizers, cold platters, and fruit displays.

Place the cocktail bars at opposite ends of the room to prevent crowding. There is usually an open bar throughout the event.

Sometimes there is dancing during the cocktail hour (or throughout the event). The guests are asked to be seated just prior to the introduction of the bar mitzvah boy into the banquet room.

Children's Room

Sometimes a separate room is set up for the children. This usually works best when the number of children under thirteen will exceed one-fifth the total number of guests.

Be sure to satisfy these children, and their parents will consider you for their future bar mitzvahs. A private bar to dispense nonalcoholic drinks, and a minibuffet of special food will help make the children's party a success.

Food like small frankfurters, meatballs, potato curls, popcorn, granola mix, soda, and juices can be served to the children. Or you can have an ice cream cart so they can create their own sundaes, complete with all the trimmings.

Other fun activities can be included for the children—from hiring an artist to draw caricatures or teach the kids balloon twisting, to magic shows and clowns.

The Introduction

The parents, siblings, and friends of the bar mitzvah boy will be seated together at the head table. The headwaiter lines the friends up first for the entry, from the shortest to the tallest. The master of ceremonies introduces them en masse as "friends of" the bar mitzvah boy.

As they enter and circle the edge of the dance floor, they are usually accompanied by lively music. Sometimes on their way to the head table, they are led by one of the musicians, Pied Piper–style.

Each place setting at the head table should have a card inscribed with a name. The boy's closest siblings, friends, or his parents can sit next to him.

Everyone stands as the master of ceremonies announces the names of the bar mitzvah boy and his parents. The boy enters with a parent on each side, and they proceed to stand in front of the cake table.

Brothers and sisters enter next, carrying a linen prayer shawl (*tallit*) that will be worn around the boy's shoulders to symbolize biblical garments. The tallit is handed to a grandparent or elder relative, who places it around the boy's shoulders. The blessing (*moitzi*) is said over the challah, which is distributed to the family. Then the headwaiter takes the rest of the challah into the kitchen to be cut and placed on platters to be offered to the rest of the guests.

Sometimes there is a candle-lighting ceremony, and the headwaiter should be prepared to distribute slender white candles to the participants.

The Dinner

You can offer several menu options for bar mitzvahs, both kosher and kosher-style. The number of courses is usually high, including an intermezzo course, and an elaborate dessert table (Viennese table) as well as the bar mitzvah cake.

The dessert table can have its own printed menu card, and includes hot and cold items: tarts, petit fours, cream puffs, *rugalah*, eclairs, napoleons, mousse, parfaits, fruit, strudel, blintzes, crepes, baked apples, and cherries jubilee. Assorted cordials, demitasse, espresso, lattes, and coffee should also be offered.

The more variety you have, the better your presentation will be received. The bar mitzvah cake is displayed along one side, but is not cut until the ceremony.

The cake cutting ceremony is typical of birthday celebrations, with the candles lit and blown out by the birthday boy. The headwaiter then cuts the cake to be plated and distributed to the guests.

• Bar Mitzvah—Meat Dinner Menu
(50–150 guests)

Cocktail hour	Assorted hot and cold hors d'oeuvres served butler style. Open bar. Champagne poured after main course.
Appetizer	Gefilte fish in natural juice, or Chopped liver pâté rosette
Entrée	Roast prime ribs of beef au jus, or Roast half chicken, with spiced peaches
	Browned potato Fresh garden peas Tossed green salad Traditional challah
Dessert	Bar Mitzvah cake, Viennese table
Beverage	Coffee, tea, punch

• Bar Mitzvah—Dairy Dinner Menu
(50–150 guests)

Cocktail hour	Assorted hot and cold canapés and hors d'oeuvres (fish, eggs, cheese, and vegetables) passed butler style. Open bar. Wine or champagne to be served with main course.
Appetizer	Chopped egg and browned onion, or Herring bits in wine
Entrée	Baked fresh salmon, or Broiled cod with wine sauce
	Parsley new potatoes Cheese blintzes with sour cream

	Asparagus spears
	Traditional challah
Dessert	Viennese table
	Bar Mitzvah cake
Beverage	Coffee, tea, punch

8 | *Outside Services*

Outside services are things that are usually incorporated into catered functions, such as photography, flowers, music, entertainment, printing, limousines, valet parking, and formal wear.

Caterers can either receive a commission for their referrals or supply these services themselves. When caterers provide outside services, they must make sure they can purchase the goods at a rate that will enable them to make a reasonable profit.

In addition, if your business chooses to supply flower arrangements and centerpieces, then you have the added responsibility of ensuring that the flowers are top quality, delivered intact, and are arranged to the client's satisfaction. This means you must handle the contractual arrangements with the outside service according to the client's specifications.

Referrals

Many caterers find that the best way to offer package plans is to include referrals for reliable outside services, letting the client handle their own contractual arrangements. The commission to your business can range from 10 to 15 percent of the customer price.

In order to give a proper referral for outside services, you'll need promotional brochures detailing various options and prices. Since most clients don't have the time to track down these services, and since theoretically the commission doesn't come out of their own pocket, they're usually willing to trust the caterer's advice. Your business receives a commission, and you are freed from any legal obligation to the client.

If you find you're making a large number of referrals, you can obtain an even better deal with your outside services by offering to make them your "house" band or flower boutique. You agree to recommend their service exclusively, and in exchange, they give you a higher commission. The outside service gets more business from you, and you get more profit from each function.

Another way to keep the price of outside services competitive is to have two or more stores you recommend. By rotating referrals among several flower shops, you may find you can get better deals for your clients.

Make sure to check on each client's satisfaction with outside services you recommend. If the service is unsatisfactory, then you must find a new provider, as their failure will reflect on your catering business.

Unfamiliar Outside Services

Some clients prefer to furnish their own outside services— their uncle is a photographer, or their friend's son has a band they want to hire.

In this case, the caterer must take special care to ensure the outside service can be coordinated properly into the function. The guests will naturally assume that the caterer supplied or recommended the outside service, and your business will suffer if they don't adhere to acceptable standards.

It can be difficult to question the quality of an outside service when the client has a personal stake in it, yet you must find out the qualifications and experience of the unfamiliar service. Often clients choose inferior, inexperienced services simply because they are low priced. Then you must point out the numerous complications that will affect the rest of the function if the outside service fails to do its job properly.

If you are truly concerned about the quality of an outside service—particularly the music or flowers—you can offer incentives to clients to help convince them to accept your recommendation. Meals for the band members, or buffet flowers offered gratis.

If you must deal with unfamiliar outside services, speak to the manager or bandleader at the time the catering contract is signed. It may be up to you to make sure they do an acceptable job. On the other hand, if this new outside service works out well, then you can offer to make recommendations to them in return for a commission.

Soliciting Referrals

Sometimes outside services can reciprocate by referring clients to your catering business. It can help your business if you become acquainted with bridal services and party planners—basically the professional networkers of catered functions. You should also consider making contact with the managers of public facilities, meeting halls, and the better hotels that have function space to rent.

Contact businesses such as:

- Bridal consultants
- Bridal shops
- Bridal registries (in department stores)
- Formalwear shops
- Photographers
- Florists
- Printers

Solicit their referrals by offering to refer them to your clients. You'll need a professional brochure for your business, and letters from satisfied clients. You can even ask that an album of your services be kept in the store for interested clients, including samples of your menus, photographs of your various functions, package plan options, serviceware options, and other outside services.

The prices should be settled for various basic packages, and the commissions arranged in advance.

Florist

Each banquet table is set up with a decorative centerpiece—usually fresh flowers. Since this will be an integral part of your presentation, you need to be actively involved in choosing the centerpieces.

The buffet is decorated with a floral centerpiece as well, unless you offer an edible centerpiece as part of your menu. You'll also need flat table ferns to spread between the dishes, and it can be a nice touch to place single flowers among the ferns. Choose flowers that can lie flat—rosebuds, lilies, baby's breath, daffodils, tulips, etc.

There are many other types of floral decorations that caterers can offer to their clients. Some may wish to provide corsages for the honored women guests. Others may want to place potted trees or hanging plants in the function room. You can also provide floral baskets, standing arrangements, garlands, candle arrangements, and floral canopies.

Centerpieces

Offer a few basic floral arrangements to go along with your package plans. Simply state at the bottom that one centerpiece per table will be included. Usually, the client specifies the color, and leaves the rest to the caterer.

The centerpieces for the banquet tables are squat and

round, set in either a square or a round base. The top can't project too high or it will block the view of people seated across from each other.

The buffet table can be decorated with a taller arrangement, and dais tables usually have one or more long, low centerpieces. Sometimes cocktail tables are decorated with bud vases holding single sprays of flowers.

Ask your florist for photos or a brochure of your centerpiece choices and other floral decorations. If your client prefers other types of flowers, you can suggest they visit the florist shop you recommend to choose their flowers. This may mean the prices will vary depending on the season and the number of blooms, but it ensures that your clients will get exactly what they want.

After the function, the emcee announces that the centerpiece may be taken by one of the guests at each table. The caterer should never remove flowers (which are the possession of the client) unless you are specifically ordered to.

Occasionally, a client will purchase the flowers separately. Your staff shouldn't deal with the transport of these arrangements, because then you would be responsible for their appearance. You can give your client a rebate on the price of the package plan, however, since you won't have to provide the flowers. Make sure to point out that you are not responsible for the quality and timeliness of these floral arrangements—a factor that can be detrimental to the caterer's reputation as well as the host's.

Music

One of the quickest ways to ruin a party is to have bad or inappropriate music. Even if the musicians are skilled, they must be able to catch the tone of the crowd and create the right music to lift the spirits of the function.

The best bands and disc jockeys work with the guests,

inviting their participation and playing all types of requested music. They also make sure to not cater to the vocal few, leaving the rest of the guests idle at their tables.

The headwaiter coordinates with the musicians in order to create a stylish function. There are customary tunes to accompany different presentations, introductions, and dances. The leader of the band (sometimes taking the role of master of ceremonies) must be conversant with the rituals and music for your function.

Bands are sometimes asked to accompany vocalists or perform special songs. Find out what kinds of music the client prefers, and hire a band that suits them, or at least, hire one that can read sheet music.

Music is optional during the cocktail hour. Some clients prefer to have a few musicians playing to warm up the room, but others feel it interferes with guests mingling prior to the function. String instruments, or a pianist with another instrument accompanying, are often preferred for cocktail parties, in order to complement the general discussion rather than overpower it.

One way to find good musicians is to get in touch with a talent agent who can provide all kinds of different music for your functions. Though an agent takes a cut of the fee (usually 15 percent), the bands are sometimes offered at cheaper rates since they are being regularly booked.

Prices

Prices are based on the number of musicians hired, by the hour. The caterer usually determines the number of musicians, depending on the size of the room.

If there is a union in your area, they will send a representative to your business to explain the local rules. Unions determine the size of the group required according to the seating capacity of each room. They will also check in regularly to make sure you're hiring only card-carrying union members, and conforming to the rules.

Bands usually play for twenty minutes, then break for ten, giving you forty minutes of music for each hour. You can also hire bands to play continuously for fifty minutes an hour, with a ten-minute break. Obviously most clients prefer continuous music, but this will cost more. The client can also arrange to have the band play a tape of prerecorded music during their breaks.

The caterer must remember to arrange with the client for the payment of the food and beverages for the band. Either these meals can be thrown in gratis, or added into the total number of guests.

Photography

An excellent photographer can be as important to the caterer as to the client. Photographs that are carefully arranged to include the caterer's elegant presentation can become a sales tool for your business, as well an important personal remembrance for the client.

You'll need to have albums from one or more photographers to show prospective clients. Once you've worked with a photographer, he or she can provide photos of your functions as part of a promotional package. Photos of wedding cakes with the happy couple, and the birthday boy ready to blow out the candles can be great showcase shots for your catering business.

Aside from the photographer's skill, the most important thing is to find people who don't intrude on the function itself. An overbearing photographer who orders people around in endless poses can bring a party to an instant halt.

Prices

Many photographers offer a package plan for weddings, bar mitzvahs, and anniversaries, specifying the number of photographs, sizes, and a variety of display albums. They can even offer portrait sittings in their studio prior to the function.

Prices are determined by the final number of prints the client selects from the contact sheet; however, many photographers require a minimum guarantee.

Make sure the contract specifies the date the contact sheet will be provided for the client, and how long it will take to get the final prints. The proofs are usually kept by the photographer, but the client can order additional prints later if they wish.

Some photographers offer full video coverage for an additional fee. This can be an ideal accompaniment to a special function, and more and more couples are taking advantage of this technology to capture their entire wedding ceremony and reception.

Limousine and Valet Services

Limousines are usually rented by the hour, for a minimum of two or three hours. You can choose between a variety of styles and colors, from a luxury sedan to a white stretch limousine complete with uniformed chauffeur. A caterer should be able to recommend a few reliable limousine services.

Valet services are essential for most catered functions—guests are arriving in their best clothes and aren't interested in walking long distances. Check the reputation of local valet services with the Better Business Bureau, and ask for letters of recommendation. Also, make sure the valet service is bonded and completely covered by insurance in case there's an accident.

Printing

There are many printed materials that the caterer can provide directly for their clients, including menus, napkins, matchbooks, and souvenirs. A caterer can create an album of sample materials, from which the client can order. These items are then purchased by the caterer and marked up for a reasonable profit.

Caterers must have their own supply of place cards that are provided free of charge to the client. These are usually done in plain print, with the table number and a line to write the name of the guest. Or place cards can be specially printed with each guest's name, and color coordinated with the menus and cocktail napkins.

Menus can be printed in a variety of ways. They usually carry your business logo at the bottom center, or one upper corner. You can also inscribe the menus with the initials of the honored guests or the hosts.

The production manager should always check the menus after receiving them to make sure there are no errors. Any printed material must be ordered far enough in advance in case you need time to correct any mistakes.

Other printed materials should be left between the client and the printer; for example, things that require special wording or arrangements like programs and forms. Other items, such as invitations, announcements, and coat-check tickets, can be either left to the client or supplied by the caterer.

9 | *Equipment*

Aside from the equipment you need to run your catering kitchen, most of the serviceware, linen, uniforms, and tables and chairs can be rented for each function. This saves you from having to purchase costly inventory when you first start your business, and ensures that you pay only for the equipment you need.

Do comparative shopping among the suppliers in your area so that you can offer your clients a variety of high quality serviceware at a reasonable price (adding a small service charge for you).

Once your catering business is doing consistent business, it may be more cost-effective to purchase the basic items yourself, such as chafing dishes, china, silverware, and glassware. But you don't have to rush into owning your own serviceware—it limits the styles you can offer clients, and ties up your money in depreciating inventory.

When you do decide to buy your own serviceware, make sure it is the highest quality.

Transport Equipment

Usually food is transported in covered wooden or plastic containers. All equipment that is used to transport the food from the catering kitchen to the site of the function should be marked with the name of your business.

When each item is packed, the container is clearly marked with the contents. The chef also inventories the food before it leaves the kitchen, and marks each item on the inventory sheet as it is loaded into the vans.

A catchall bag should be taken to each function, containing things you may need during setup or in case of emergencies. Since appearance is everything in your banquet presentation, make sure you have thumbtacks for table skirting, straight pins, cellophane and masking tape, string, corkscrews, bottle openers, knives, a staple gun, extension cords, and a basic tool kit.

It's also a good idea for the banquet manager to have at least $100 petty cash in case of emergencies. You may have to send someone for food, equipment, or liquor that you forgot to purchase.

Banquet Room Furniture

At one time or another a catering business will need to rent different size tables, dance floors, band platforms, speaker's rostrums, and room dividers. When you provide banquet room furniture, you must be sure you have the right hand trucks and dollies to transport it to the function site. Bars are usually made of formica, and come with large rollers for easy transport.

Chairs are usually stacked in units of ten. The bottom of the legs must be capped with rubber or plastic to prevent scratching or rug damage. Padded foam rubber seats are preferable because they offer the most comfort for your guests.

Don't forget the usefulness of room screens. They can be used to cover unattractive areas at the function site, such as the kitchen setup, or exit doors that aren't in use.

When you purchase furniture, make sure it is durable since you'll be using it frequently. Yet it must be attractive enough to please the eye. You'll also want furniture that is lightweight and easy to transport, such as folding tables and chairs. But make sure they are sturdy when erected.

Tables

Round banquet tables are very popular because they are easy to move, and provide equal access for conversation among the seated guests.

Most banquet tables have a vinyl pad or cloth covering to make their surfaces silent. Wishbone legs are preferable because they give the most under-table space to guests. And check the locking devices on the legs, to make sure they are secure when set.

Approximately five feet should be left between the tables for adequate aisle space. To get the most seating out of a room, stagger the rows. Round tables come in sizes 36, 42, 48, 54, 60, 66, 72, and 84 inches in diameter.

Oval tables create a larger seating capacity, so for smaller function areas they may be your best option. Oval tables come in sizes 72×36, 72×48, 84×48, and 96×48 inches.

Rectangular tables can be joined together in many different shapes. But remember, these arrangements aren't as conducive to conversation among the guests, and should be reserved for meetings or awards ceremonies. You can arrange rectangular tables in a "U"-shaped set up, "T" shape, "I" shape, "E" shape, or "O" shape.

The most common sizes for rectangular tables are 30 inches wide, and either four, five, six, or eight feet long. Classroom style tables are 18 inches wide, and usually seat people only along one side.

Table size	Seating capacity	Linen size
36" diameter	4	$54'' \times 54''$
42" diameter	6	$60'' \times 60''$
48" diameter	8	$64'' \times 64''$

54" diameter	8	72" × 72"
60" diameter	10	72" × 72"
72" diameter	12	90" × 90"
48" × 30"	4 (or a tight 6)	54" × 72"
60" × 30"	6	54" × 84"
72" × 30"	8	54" × 108"
96" × 30"	8 or 10	54" × 120"

Linen

By renting your linen, you can offer your clients a large selection of colors and styles, while cutting down on the expensive upkeep. All linen must be washed, dried, ironed, and properly folded after every use. It's usually much more economical to rent linen on a per-function basis.

Get samples that you can show your clients. Some of the popular colors for linen are: yellow, gold, beige, brown, red, pink, lilac, light blue, dark blue, green, purple, and black. Mixing the colors with white linen, you can create unique effects in your banquet presentation. However, with formal service, white or very pastel linens should be used.

These days, linen is really made from a heavy cotton fabric. Ask your suppliers what other fabrics and patterns they offer. Lace overlays are popular, especially for weddings. And nylon or net covers can be used for the buffet and cake tables.

Skirting is the material that goes around the edge of the table to hide the legs. Then the tablecloth drapes over the skirting. Skirting comes in different lengths for different size tables:

48" diameter	13 feet
60" diameter	16 feet
72" diameter	19 feet
72" × 30"	12 feet
96" × 30"	14 feet

You can usually rent uniforms for your service personnel and kitchen staff from the same place you rent your linen. Or you can hire service staff from a temporary agency that supplies its own uniforms.

For each function, you'll also have to order an extra number of white service napkins for your waiters. Other kitchen linen you will need include:

1. potholders that are large and heavy-duty;
2. dish towels for wiping pots and pans;
3. hand towels for cleanup, and wiping down serviceware before use;
4. mop-up rags to handle spills, dirty equipment, and floors.

Tents

You can rent outdoor equipment the same way you rent serviceware and linen. When renting tents, make sure the company is reliable and bonded, in case their workmen damage the function site while setting up the tent.

The tent must be erected on level, firm ground. You can instruct the deliverers on where to put each of the protective coverings, creating a smooth flow for the party.

If possible, request flaps to cover guests in case of bad weather. And you can offer to color-coordinate the tents with the color scheme of the party.

Have the supplier set up the tents the day before, rather than the morning of the function. This will give you time enough to set up the tables and chairs.

Order the correct tent size for the number of guests that are expected:

Tent size	Seating capacity
14' × 14'	25
16' × 16'	30
12' × 25'	35

Tent size	Seating capacity
20' × 20'	40
20' × 25'	50
30' × 30'	90
40' × 40'	160
50' × 75'	375

Serviceware

The serviceware includes china, silverware, glassware, and serving pieces. Be sure to pick options that are distinctive, suiting your clientele and menus.

When buying serviceware, determine the maximum seating capacity of your business, and factor in breakage and loss. If you can, go for a higher grade of serviceware that has interchangeable pieces—a dessert plate that is the same as the salad plate. And make sure replacements can be quickly obtained when you needed them.

Serving Pieces

You'll want to offer at least several "show" pieces for your clients to chose from—such as an elaborate punch bowl, coffee urn, or standing champagne bucket for each table.

When you first purchase serviceware, choose items that can be figured by table rather than per person, such as sugar bowls, salt and pepper shakers, oil and vinegar carafes.

Stainless steel takes much less maintenance than silver, and is easier to wash and sanitize. It also resists scratching much more than silver. Yet there's nothing like gorgeous pieces of silver, and with a little extra time and expense, your serving pieces could become the perfect complement to your banquet presentation.

Standard serving pieces and accessories are:

plate covers	to fit dinner and showplate
platters w/covers	18″ or 24″ in length

soup tureens	ten-portion
vegetable dishes	two-compartment (twenty portions)
gravy/sauce boats	15 oz.
bread/relish trays	10″ in length
ice buckets	7″ in diameter
water pitchers	54 oz.
coffee pots	54 oz.
teapots	11 oz.
punch bowls	5 gal.
sugar bowls	7 oz.
creamers	7 oz.
ashtrays	4″

You also need the proper serving spoons and forks for each food item, plus sauce and gravy boats, carving tools, and dressing containers.

Chafing Dishes

Chafing dishes consist of a frame, water pan, insert, cover, and fuel holder. If you serve buffets, you'll need chafing dishes that are attractive, rather than simply serviceable.

The base should be filled with approximately one inch of water, leaving enough room for the top insert. The canned fuel for the chafing dishes is ignited fifteen minutes before the food is placed into the dishes to ensure that the water reaches the boiling point.

Flatware

Flatware is the forks, spoons, and knives. Most flatware is made of sterling silver, silver (or gold) plate, or stainless steel. Whether you buy or rent flatware, make sure it is comfortable to use. The quality of your food won't be appreciated if the dining experience is awkward.

Sterling silver is extremely expensive, and probably not worth the effort unless you specialize in fancy formal functions. There are also different degrees of silver-plating, so make sure yours is durable enough to last through repeated uses and washing.

Or you can buy stainless steel flatware. It comes in just as many elegant patterns as silver, and has the advantage of being easy to maintain.

Flatware consists of:

1. knives—dinner, butter, steak, fruit, cheese;
2. forks—dinner, salad, dessert, cocktail;
3. spoons—coffee, dessert, soup, iced tea.

Glassware

The design of your glassware should complement your china and flatware. Clear glassware is most commonly used; however, you can use tinted glass to make your table presentation stand out. Make sure this doesn't conflict with your client's preferred color scheme.

Avoid buying fragile glassware. When you do purchase glassware, get a glass rack to help prevent breakage during transport.

At the function, when you wash the glasses, use a separate tub of water from the china and flatware. This will ensure that your glasses are sparkling clean, and will cut down on breakage.

Standard sizes:

water goblet	10 oz.
iced tea	12 oz.
fruit juice	5 oz.
wine	
red	9 oz.
white	7 oz.
Champagne	
saucer	5 1/2 ox.
tulip	6 1/2 oz.

punch cups	4 oz.
beer	10 oz.
cocktail	3 oz.
highball	8 oz.
whiskey sour	4 oz.
Tom Collins	12 oz.
liqueur	3 oz.
brandy snifter	8 oz.
sherry	3 oz.
port	4 oz.
shot	1 oz.

China

The color and pattern of the china should enhance the appearance of the food. Simple patterns hold the widest appeal, but that doesn't mean you should rent or purchase something that is familiar to the eye. Since catered functions are special occasions, the guests expect to see something different from the china at their grandmother's house.

When purchasing china, it's best to stick to one pattern until your business is larger. And make sure the pieces are easily replaceable, and of medium weight, with rolled edges to prevent chipping.

Sample Equipment List

A sample equipment list for a wedding for 150 guests would be as follows:

1	gazebo (white)	40′ × 40′
1	dance floor	20′ × 20′
4	platforms	4′ × 8′ × 12″ (two for head table, two for band)
2	steps	3′ × 6″
2	electric extensions (for band and kitchen)	
1	tent (peach)	40′ × 40′

Tables

18	round (ban-quet)	60″
15	round (cocktail)	30″
12	rectangle	72″ × 30″ (for bridal table, buffet, bars)
5	rectangle	60″ × 30″ (for kitchen, gifts)
2	square	40″ × 40″ (wedding cake, name/place display)
160	chairs (white, cushion)	

Dishes (white, with silver trim)

165	plates	12″ (10 percent overage for staff and breakage)
	entrée	11″
	appetizer	6″
	dessert	6″
	soup bowls	8″
165	cups	
	saucers	

Silverware (Empire style)

160	forks (entrée)
	salad
	dessert
160	spoons (coffee)
	soup
40	sugar spoons
160	knives
	butter knives
1	bridal knife

Glassware (rose-tint)

180	water
180	champagne

200 highball
100 old-fashioned
50 cocktail
50 beer
10 shot

Serviceware

40 salt & pepper (two per table, two per bar)
40 ashtrays (one per banquet table, per cocktail
     table, two per bar)
8   water pitchers
20 sugar & creamer (one per table, two per bridal
     table)
1   coffee urn 250-cup
1   hot water urn 60-cup
8   server's trays
8   tray stands
4   corkscrews
4   can/bottle openers
4   plastic tubs for ice

Kitchen pots and serving utensils provided by the catering kitchen

Linen Order

20 round (white) 90"
15 rectangle 54" × 108" (for bridal table, buffet,
     bars)
20 square (peach) 64" × 64" (wedding cake, gift,
     cocktail)
     prepleated skirting (white) 140'
160 dinner napkins (peach)
40 service napkins (white)

Uniforms

8   waiters' jackets (two small, three medium, three large)
3   chefs' hats
4   chefs' coats, shirts, pants (one small, two medium, 1 large)
12 aprons (white)
24 kitchen towels

10 | *The Catering Kitchen*

The layout of your catering kitchen is very important. It needs to be efficient for the types of food production your business specializes in. The chef (the person in charge of food preparation) should be directly involved in making decisions on the practical setup of the kitchen.

The preparation and cooking areas are the focus of the kitchen, with easy access to waste disposal, storage rooms, and washing stations. Tables and work surfaces should be left mobile so they can be shifted depending on the preparation at hand. This will keep employees moving in a smooth flow, rather than creating cross-traffic.

The aisles should be wide enough to allow passage, but not so spacious as to create difficulty when moving food from one station to the next. You should factor in the open doors when calculating the aisle space.

Though kitchens are typically bare floored, you might consider laying down some cushy rubber mats that can be washed when needed. This will reduce fatigue in your chefs. It also helps to have nonglare surfaces on the counters.

Equipment

Essentials for a catering kitchen include: good lighting with protected bulbs, fans for ventilation, a fire prevention system, fire extinguisher, and proper floor drainage. The sinks need to be large enough to accommodate the largest equipment, and fill things like your coffee urn and soup kettles.

You'll also need spice racks, bins for raw ingredients such as flour, sugar, salt, rice, etc. And mounted can openers, mixers, slicers, choppers, graters, and grinders. Other common equipment you may need are deep fryers, vegetable steamers, steam kettles, waffle bakers, toasters, and toaster ovens with automatic timers.

The kitchen must have sufficient amounts and sizes of roasting pans, frying pans, pots, and kettles to handle the cooking load. Most frequently used equipment should be closest to hand—either hung in the first rows or placed on the shelves easiest to reach.

For a beginning catering business, you can purchase most of your equipment (from heavy ranges to slicers) secondhand from the same supply stores that sell new equipment.

Ranges and Ovens

You'll need enough roasting and oven space to prepare the volume of food you sell. This depends on the type of menus you offer.

In the beginning, your business will likely need only one range-oven combination. But configure your kitchen space to add another range and/or oven once business increases.

Position the ovens to avoid excessive walking or awkward stooping. The broiler is a slow-cooking operation, so it doesn't need to be centrally placed like stovetops.

At least once a week, all ranges and ovens should be cleaned thoroughly, with regular maintenance between uses. If cleaned properly, your heavy equipment will operate more efficiently and last much longer.

Prep Areas

Most catering businesses purchase their meat already dressed, but depending on the expertise of your chef, you may need a meat preparation area. This includes: meat blocks, adequate sink and drainboard facilities, butchering tools, and portion scales.

At the very least, your business will need a good meat slicer. This ensures exact portions are obtained from each cut of meat. The slicer should be easy to clean, and must be cleaned after each use, or dangerous bacteria will grow on the blades.

You will also need enough surface space in your kitchen to prepare salads and vegetables. These areas are ideally placed next to sinks and drainboards where the produce can be washed, rinsed, and dried before being cut. Wire baskets, salad spinners, and racks can be used for drainage.

If baking is done on-premises, it's best to establish a separate area and a separate oven for your baked goods. However, since most baking equipment is specialized and preparation takes large amounts of time, most caterers purchase their baked goods fresh from a local baker.

Storage

Storing your raw ingredients will require specialized types of equipment. Depending on your menus, preparation times, and volume of production, you'll need different storage methods for your business.

Dry storage and refrigeration storage spaces are usually about the same size. Your storerooms should have enough shelving to clearly display your inventory of goods.

In dry storage, there must be plenty of space between and under shelves for proper ventilation. The room can't be too warm or damp, or the goods will spoil. Raised platforms or flats will keep food bins off the floor.

It also helps to have a table in each storage area with scales, packaging materials, and inventory check-in/check-out lists.

Refrigerators

You'll need a large amount of refrigerator space because most food that is partially prepared or waiting for transport to the function site must be stored in a refrigerator.

You can buy secondhand refrigerators, which will limit the expense, until you are sure of what your catering business requires. Refrigerators come in different sizes, including: uprights, chests, cabinets, freezers, and walk-ins.

Refrigerators must be kept at the proper temperatures to prevent food spoilage. An alarm system can be attached to maintain the temperature, and there are automatic defrosting units that prevent ice buildup on the cooling units.

Just as in dry storage, there must be enough ventilation space between the shelves. It's also a good idea to have separate areas for milk and cheese storage that's away from the fish and meat.

Washing Area

If you can, purchase automated equipment that will speed up the cleaning and sterilization of your serviceware. It also allows dishes and pans to be protectively racked and stacked throughout the washing procedure.

Pot washing requires deep sinks, with large enough areas for cooling and drainage. You also need a prerinsing and scraping area. The garbage disposal should be located in this sink, and to reduce the amount of ground waste, place trash bins here as well.

The shelving and storage space for serviceware can be located in the washing area. The cleaning supplies, brooms, mops, and other equipment can also be dried and stored in this area. Pots and pans should be stored within easy reach of the kitchen staff.

Hand sinks must also be provided so that kitchen employees can easily and frequently wash their hands.

Receiving and Docking Area

Your catering kitchen will need a platform or adequate space allocated to receive food when it is delivered by the trucks. You should also have a large-scale setup in this area, for quick checks on bulk sizes.

The receiving space must be adequate to set out the goods for examination, with a tabletop surface for handling invoices. The goods will be taken from this entry location to their proper storage places.

11 | *Purchasing Food*

Judicious food purchasing can make or break your catering business. It takes knowledge of food preparation and storage to have the necessary ingredients always on hand, without backing up inventory.

The purchasing should be done by one person, either the production manager, chef, or menu planner. The purchaser will have to frequent the markets, and become knowledgeable about current rates and supplies. Try to feature produce and other food products that are plentiful in your area. Fresh food will always taste the best.

Ideally, your purchaser is constantly bargain shopping, with the added handicap of having to predict food items that will be readily available on the market in several weeks or months.

The purchaser must also maintain inventory and ensure proper storage of all ingredients. A record should be kept of purchase orders and your current supply, as well as invoices, market quotes, and sales contacts.

Ordering

A purchase form is filled out for all orders that are placed, ensuring that proper records are kept. The original copy is sent to the purveyor, with one copy returned to the purchaser (or the chef, if he supervises the receiving clerk). The third copy goes to accounting, so they can make sure the menu prices they are quoting are accurate.

The ordering should be done after the precise number of guests has been finalized. The purchaser works with the chef to reduce waste that occurs with particular items. Overordering is one of the easiest ways to lose significant amounts of your profit margin.

The purchaser should therefore be familiar with how many portions can be obtained from each measure of food. For some salad recipes, a head of lettuce will serve six people—for others, it will serve eight. Cuts of meat also need to be measured accurately.

However, to guard against running short because of uninvited guests, spillage, or seconds, you can purchase a certain extra percentage for each function. If there are 100 guests invited, then add 10 percent more than the ingredients that are needed. For a larger number of guests, this percentage can be lowered. This buffer can be figured into the total cost when you're determining the price per guest.

A sample order list could be broken into categories:

1. *Meat and Fish*—prime rib (16 slices per rib), cold turkey slices, bacon
2. *Bakery*—birthday cake (vanilla cake with lemon frosting), dinner rolls
3. *Produce*—parsley garnish, onions, celery, cherry tomatoes, potatoes, strawberries, grapes, pineapple, cantaloupe, honeydew melon
4. *Dairy*—milk, half & half, butter, eggs, blue cheese
5. *Grocery*—black pepper, salt, sage, paprika, vegetable oil, olive oil, flour, wine vinegar, horseradish, sugar, sugar substitutes, sugar cubes, lemon juice, pineapple juice, tea bags, coffee, decaffeinated coffee, beef stock
6. *Beverage*—tomato juice, orange juice, ginger ale,

cola, lemon-lime, diet cola, club soda, tonic,
sparkling water
7. *Liquor*—scotch, gin, rye, bourbon, vodka, rum,
domestic and imported beer (regular and light),
white and red wine, champagne for toasts
8. *Paper goods*—plastic wrap, aluminum foil,
cocktail napkins, toothpicks, take-home
containers, 8″ doilies

Receiving

Deliveries are usually made during certain hours. The
person who does the receiving should inspect all of the
delivered goods, comparing the quantities, measure, weight,
and price of each item against your copy of the purchase
order. The receiver also checks and approves the quality of
food.

If anything is wrong with the order, the receiver must
bring it immediately to the attention of the vendor
representative or salesperson. The goods shouldn't be
accepted until they concur with purchase orders and
specifications.

When the goods are accepted, the signed invoice should
be turned over to the accountant.

12 | *Pricing a Menu*

When you price a menu, you must take into account all of the costs: purchasing and preparing the food, storage, renting equipment, transport, setup, employee wages, cleanup, and your business overhead.

When you first start a catering business, it may be easiest to base your menu prices on competitors' offers. But if you know exactly where your money is going, then small adjustments in your menu or better supplier prices can quickly multiply into profits.

Make sure you have all the specifications before quoting a price for any function.

1. The menu must be broken down into the necessary ingredients and portions according to the number of guests. Liquor costs should also be estimated.
2. Equipment and linen lists should be prepared, covering the costs of everything you need to rent.
3. Employee work schedules and pay rates should be created that will cover the needs of the function from preparation to cleanup.
4. Transportation and overhead costs must also be added.

Pricing Menu Ingredients

The chef needs to establish standard recipes and get an exact portion cost for each food item. You have to factor in losses during preparation and cooking, so make some sample batches to test how many portions you get from each. You'll need to have precise portion measurements, and make sure the kitchen staff pre-plates the meal using the appropriate ladles.

The price of condiments, sauces, spices, and garnishes should be added to the cost of the food items they accompany. This includes the cost of rolls, butter, cream, sugar, coffee, tea, and milk.

You'll also have to factor in a certain extra percentage in case of additional guests, employee meals, spillage, and accidents.

Overhead

To arrive at the cost of overhead, you must calculate the following items:

1. rent for catering kitchen and function rooms;
2. utilities: electricity, heat, water, gas, garbage removal, telephone;
3. permits, licenses, taxes, insurance;
4. breakage and depreciation of equipment;
5. professional fees (lawyers, accountant);
6. advertising and promotional materials;
7. repairs and maintenance;
8. equipment rental for the catering kitchen (linen, serviceware, uniforms, etc.);
9. cleaning supplies and paper goods;
10. salaries for nonfunction personnel (salesperson, administrative staff).

By adding together the operating costs, you can determine your monthly overhead figure. Then break this figure down according to the number of meals you serve each month. This will give you an average flat rate to add to each function in order to cover overhead.

Determining Menu Prices

To determine your menu price, you first determine your
total food cost. For a dinner for 100 guests, the costs are as
follows:

		× the number of
Item	Cost per portion	portions (100)
appetizer	$ .28	$ 28.00
salad	.24	24.00
entrée	1.95	95.00
vegetable	.18	18.00
potato	.18	18.00
dessert	.32	32.00
coffee	.15	15.00
rolls, etc.	.20	20.00
Total	$3.42	$342.00

Then you determine the labor costs (gratuities added later):

4 food prep cooks at $50	=	$200
6 waiters at $30	=	180
1 bartender at $40	=	40
2 kitchen help at $25	=	50
1 chef at $60	=	60
1 banquet manager at $60	=	60
Total payroll expenses	=	$590

Then you add together the food, labor, and overhead cost:

total food	$342.00	
total labor	590.00	
overhead	500.00	= Total cost $1,432.00

To reach the total menu price, you must add a reasonable
profit for your business (1/3 to 1/4 the total cost):

total cost $1,432.00		
profit	450.00	=	$1882.00 or $19 per person

When you create package plans, you must include the cost of equipment rental, outside services, liquor, room rental, and gratuities. For the wedding menu that was broken down above, your business could end up charging $75 per person for a complete package plan.

Hourly Rates

It's easier to charge per hour for things like cocktail parties and open bars. The per hour rate can be reduced if additional hours are needed, on the assumption that less food and liquor will be served per hour if the party is longer. One example of an hourly price structure is:

	½ hour	1 hour	2 hours	3 hours	4 hours
Hors d'oeuvres					
butler style	$ 2.25	$ 4.00	$ 6.00	$ 8.00	$ 9.00
buffet	8.00	10.00	15.00	18.00	22.00
Open bar	$ 3.50	$ 6.00	$ 9.00	$11.00	$12.00
Gratuity (15 percent)					
Sales tax (8 percent)					
Total food and beverages per person:					
butler style	$ 7.00	$12.50	$18.00	$22.00	$26.00
buffet	14.00	20.00	30.00	35.00	38.00

Deposit

Clients make deposits to hold certain dates until a contract is signed. To record each deposit, you'll need a form to fill out which is signed by you and the client. You need the following specifications at the time of the deposit:

Current date:
Client's name, address, and phone number:
Type of function:
Day, date, and time of function:
Style of function:

Approximate number of guests:
Location of function:
Amount of deposit:
Approximate price (subject to change):

Contract

The contract is signed approximately one month prior to the event. At this time, the caterer and client finalize:

1. the number of guests that will be at the function;
2. a fully detailed and priced list of outside services and "extras" (this is usually a good time to sell extras services to go along with the total package);
3. a fixed price per head according to current market prices and the specifications of the client.

Caterers generally require a five- to seven-day notice on any changes of the final guarantees. Some caterers insist that the client pay for the number of guests' meals that are prepared, even if fewer people actually attend. Other caterers give a 5 percent leeway in the number of guests a client can have either above or below the guarantee.

Fifty percent of the total is usually payable upon signing the contract. The other half is paid on the day of the function.

If a function is canceled, a caterer may impose penalties by either refusing to refund the deposit or by charging the client for expenses incurred up to that point, as well as damages for having tied up a booking date. Whatever your business practices are, be sure to stipulate the deadlines and penalties on the contract, and go over them clearly with your potential clients.

On the other hand, what if you have to cancel a function? Say your catering kitchen gets flooded, or the roads are snowed in. If disaster strikes and it is impossible for your business to fulfill the contract, you'll need to have an act-of-God cancellation clause in the contract to cover yourself.

Overtime Charges

The contract should include overtime rates, particularly when it comes to large, festive functions like weddings and bar mitzvahs, which can go on for hours. Most caterers allow five hours for these functions, but if the party continues at the request of the client, you must be sure you'll be adequately compensated.

Either an additional charge can be made for each guest ($2 per person, per hour) or you could charge separately for liquor and labor. For example, you may have to pay $150 in overtime fees to waiters and bartenders, and six additional bottles of liquor (at $25 a bottle) are served, bringing the total overtime charges to $300.

Separate overtime charges may need to be paid for the band, parking attendants, function rooms, etc.

Contract Specifications

When making a contract with a client, be sure to specify the final number of guests, the floor plan of the function room and kitchen area, a detailed menu, and the time the function begins.

First, there must be space for the basic specifications:

Client's name, address, and telephone:
Type of function:
Function date:
Time:
Estimated number of guests:
Price per guest:
Deposit:
Final guarantee:

You'll also need the following details:

Cocktail hour
    length (1, 2, 3 hours)
    style (butler or buffet)
    bar (open or cash)
    number of hors d'oeuvres per person
    ratio of hot and cold hors d'oeuvres
    where the cocktail hour will be held (banquet area or
    separate)
Dinner
    style (sit-down or buffet)
    extra dinners (for band and photographer)
    liquor service (number of bars needed)
    serviceware requirements (extras like punch bowls,
    fountains)
    linen requirements (colors, styles)
    uniform requirements
    number of tables and chairs (seating arrangement)
    place cards
    equipment needed
Outside services
Parking and checking
Additional charges for overtime

Contract Stipulations

As far as the form of the contract goes, put the specifications of the client and the function on the front, and the conditions of the contract on the back. A lawyer should make sure your business contract conforms to local laws, but in general the following stipulations can be listed:

1. The client grants the caterer the right to make reasonable substitutions on the menu or for other items listed in the contract in order to meet increased costs for food and beverages.
2. Terms of payment—a total of half (50 percent) of the estimated bill for the function is due upon

signing the contract, with full payment due on the day of the function. Only cash, money order, or certified check will be accepted. No credit cards or personal checks.

3. Deposits are nonrefundable.
4. No outside food or liquor is permitted at the function without the consent of the banquet manager, with fees to be stipulated at that time.
5. If the function exceeds the allotted time, overtime charges will be incurred by the client.
6. The banquet manager reserves the right to cancel this agreement without notice and without liability in the event the stipulations of this contract have been violated by the client.
7. The management of the facility where the function takes place assumes all responsibility for any damages, losses, and bodily injury caused by catering personnel or guests at the function.
8. The caterer will pay all federal, state, and municipal taxes which may be applicable on services rendered.
9. Final guarantee of number of persons must be given not later than seven (7) days in advance.
10. This agreement is not assignable.

The menu should be stated as follows:

Eight assorted hors d'oeuvres and canapés per person, served butler style from 7:00 P.M. to 8:00 P.M. Dinner includes: cold borscht, roast prime rib of beef, oven-roasted cheese potatoes, coleslaw, two-tiered birthday cake, assorted minipastries (two per guest), and nonalcoholic beverages (coffee, tea, soda, juice, and sparkling water).

Liquor

The client will purchase all liquor needed for the bar, according to a list prepared by the caterer. Drinks will be served on an unlimited basis throughout the function (from 7:00 P.M. to 11:00 P.M.). The caterer will supply all the mixers and sodas needed for the bar.

Equipment

The tables, chairs, and serviceware will be provided by the caterer.

Linen

White tablecloths and pale pink napkins. White drapes on the gift and cake tables.

Labor

Includes 4 servers, 1 bartender, 2 cooks, 2 utility people (including transport), 1 headwaiter/organizer; totaling 10 employees.

Printing

Menus, on pale pink card stock. (You can also do matches, table number cards, individual place cards.)

Flowers

1 large and 8 medium, red, pink, and white floral centerpieces.

Music

The client will rent a violinist to play during dinner.

Miscellaneous

Any additional charges will be itemized on the client's final bill, agreed to by signature.

Taxes

8 percent of total food and beverages.

At the bottom of the contract, it should be stated that the above prices and times are subject to additional stipulations listed on the reverse side. You also need a space for both the caterer and the client to sign at the bottom. The complete menus and liquor inventory can be printed on separate, attached sheets.

13 | *Banquet Bar*

The main thing to remember when purchasing liquor is to buy only top quality brands. If you must cut costs, don't do it with the liquor—people will notice, and they won't like it.

Offer a wide selection of the best name brands, and if premium brands are requested, an additional charge can be added. You should never agree to purchase cheaper brands, or allow the client to supply their own liquor unless it is up to your standards.

Your primary interest in offering a banquet bar is to provide a large number of guests with drinks. If a bartender must create mixtures, an additional barkeep is suggested. Or drinks such as whiskey sours and martinis can be sold on a premixed basis. Otherwise, exotic or fancy drinks should be avoided unless they are showcased as part of your banquet presentation.

Liquor may be offered as an open or hosted bar, which is charged to the client according to the number of guests present, and the hours the bar is open. The billing can be on a consumption rate, or flat fee.

Or a cash bar can be provided by the caterer, with the guests paying for each drink. For some clients, you can charge a labor and transport fee for providing the bar, or if the gathering has large enough revenue potential, you can offer the bar gratis. However, cash bars will inevitably serve less liquor than open bars.

Estimating Consumption

It's easy to accurately estimate the amount of liquor, wine, beer, and ice you'll need for each function. Consumption depends on the number of guests, the type of function, and the number of hours it lasts. You can also take advice from your clients as to the known drinking preferences of their guests.

Based on average drinking groups of mixed men and women, the average number of drinks per person (1 1/2 oz.):

1st hour	2 1/2 to 3 drinks
2nd hour	1 1/2 drinks
3rd hour	1 drink
4th hour	1/2 drink
5th hour	1/4 drink

So, for a five-hour affair, each guest will consume almost six drinks at 1 1/2 oz. each. Multiply this by the number of guests, and you'll get the number of ounces of liquor you'll need.

Your wine ratio will usually be five white wines to one red wine served from the bar. For a party of 100 guests, you'll need approximately ten bottles of white wine, and two bottles of red. Or you can figure by the ounce—each person will consume on average two glasses of wine (5 oz. each) with their meal. Most bottles hold just over 25 oz.

Beer consumption is generally less at open bars than at cash bars. You should include a domestic, a light, and an imported beer. At outdoor functions, it's acceptable to provide kegs of beer. Otherwise, always serve bottled beer.

Soda consumption is based on a three-to-one ration of soda to liquor. If twenty liters of liquor are needed, then sixty liters (five cases, with twelve bottles a case) are needed. Preferred sodas are: cola, club, ginger ale, tonic, lemon-lime, and assorted diet sodas. If a large number of children will be present, you'll need more soda than average.

As for ice, figure you'll need about two pounds per person, depending on the beverages you offer and the weather.

Pricing Liquor

You will probably have to purchase a license to sell liquor, but it's worth it for your business. Liquor sales are highly profitable.

You can either price your liquor by the bottle or by the drink. When priced by the bottle, a bottle sales-check should be made out by the headwaiter, and is shown to the client before and after the function. If any liquor is left over, you can charge the client by the tenth of the bottle.

To determine the number of drinks obtained from each bottle, divide the bottle capacity by the ounces of liquor needed for each drink. To determine the selling price per drink, you divide the cost of the bottle by the number of drinks you can get per bottle.

Then figure in a 1/2 oz. loss due to spillage and overpour. Then add the cost of mixers, sodas, and garnishes (averaged cost per drink).

This will give you the exact cost of each drink. Then you average out the costs within the groups of drinks. For example, mixed drinks might be priced at $3.25, while straight drinks would cost $2.25. Or you can charge $2.75 for all drinks, while wine, beer, soda, and champagne would each be priced differently.

Wine is usually marked up from two to four times the cost of the bottle. You can make a good profit by offering your clients a wine list of about a dozen wines you can buy wholesale. Special or more expensive wines can be offered upon request. A nice touch is to offer the client a free bottle of the wine when you sign the contract, to ensure they are completely satisfied by the choice.

Open Bar

The open bar offers simplicity to everyone involved—clients like the effect of a free-flowing bar, and the cost is planned out in advance. If you offer beer and wine as well, it will reduce the amount of hard liquor that is consumed.

Flat Rates

There are different ways to calculate the number of drinks a client may wish to provide. Some clients may want to purchase a fixed number per guest—for example, two drinks an hour. With fifty guests, and the average cost for drinks at $2.50, the total is (50 × 2 × $2.50 = $250 an hour).

Reduced rates can be given to cocktail parties that last beyond an hour, on the premise that customers will consume less food and liquor if the party lasts longer.

In order to make sure you're not losing money on open bars, have the bartender inventory exactly how much liquor was actually consumed at each function. The cost of the alcohol is then compared to the revenue received. You'll find that it's simply not cost-effective to offer flat rates to certain groups of people (such as bachelor parties, and certain social clubs).

Consumption Rate

When an open bar is billed on a consumption basis, the client is charged for exactly the amount of liquor that is consumed. This is best for clients with a small budget, who want to control or limit the amount of liquor that is served.

First, a number of drinks is predetermined and specified in the contract. There should also be a charge for labor if the liquor revenue doesn't reach a guaranteed amount. You don't want to be hit with the cost of bartender services, when you sold only thirty drinks.

At the function, if the specified amount of liquor is served, the banquet manager quietly informs the client that the supply has been depleted. The client then decides whether to close the bar, or agrees to add additional liquor to his bill. You must be quite clear prior to the event that the liquor allowance could run short, and be prepared with a liquor request form that the headwaiter can present for the host's signature.

Don't ever rely on the authorization of a client's spouse or family member, or executives of the client if it's a business function. You must have the same signature that is on the original contract for your bill to be official.

Prior to the cocktail hour, the client should be shown the number of full bottles, and the number of empty or partially full bottles immediately after the cocktail hour is over, in order to avoid disagreement over the amount of liquor that was consumed. The soda, mixers, juices, and garnishes can be added into the price of the bottle, or charged separately on a consumption basis.

Some clients prefer to issue drink tickets, which the bartender collects with each drink that is served. Then the client is charged according to the number of tickets that were collected.

Purchasing Liquor

The area you live in will determine which liquors are preferred. In some places, scotch, bourbon, and rum are the drinks of choice, while in others, vodka, gin, and tequila may be consumed more often.

Since liquor is nonperishable, you'll cover yourself if you overstock your bars until you start to see the consumption pattern among the different types of functions.

Generally, people prefer light, dry, younger wines with their meals. But it is not necessary to match only white wine with fish or red wine with meat. However, rosé and white wines must be served chilled.

Sweet and dry vermouth are needed only if cocktails such as martinis and manhattans are requested. If straight drinks are to be served, you don't have to bother.

Even if your client pays a consumption rate for the bar, keep extra bottles on hand. If there is a run on vodka, you can replace scotch bottles with additional vodka, keeping the same number of total bottles on hand. Or there might be a run on a particular brand.

Any adjustments should be quietly brought to the attention of the client. And keep track of the amount of liquor consumed at each function so you'll have a better idea of what to stock in the future.

Setting Up the Banquet Bar

The cocktail hour is the caterer's first chance to make a good impression. For many clients, the quality of your bar service will greatly determine their satisfaction with your functions.

First, make sure there are enough bars for the number of guests that are expected—lines or sloppy service instantly make for a bad experience.

You must also serve drinks made to standard, otherwise the guests will feel cheated by a low pour, or overpowered by strong drinks.

The bar should be set up no later than fifteen minutes prior to the start of the function. This will ensure that the bar is ready for even the early arrivals. Or if there is something missing, the bartender will have time to get it.

Since the bartender's gratuity is included in the contract, you shouldn't allow tipping jars or glasses on the bar. This will make the guests feel as if they should be paying money (even if it's only a tip) when they ought to feel the liquor is flowing freely.

Bartenders

Usually, you should provide one bartender for every fifty to seventy-five guests. Add one bar backup at larger parties to help the bartender. The backup fetches ice, provides clean glasses, and assists the bartender in preparing drinks. Often there is an initial rush at the bar, during which several servers could help the bartenders as backups.

Bartenders should know how to mix all the popular drinks. Create a chart with the exact measurements of each drink, and provide the right measured pourers—1 ¼ oz. of liquor for standard drinks, and 1 ¾ oz. for cocktails.

The bartenders should be dressed in clean uniforms at all times, and should not eat or drink while behind the bar. Glassware is handled by the stem or base, never on the rim of the glass. Ashtrays should be kept clean.

When dealing with intoxicated guests, it's best to have the bartender alert the banquet manager, who can properly deal with the matter.

And as for bartenders, the list of nevers are:

- never leave the bar unattended;
- never serve minors;
- never question the guests—if something isn't good enough, instantly make a new drink.

Bar Equipment

When you're stocking a banquet bar, you'll need:
A portable bar, bar glassware, two sets of salt and pepper shakers, two strainers, mixing spoons, pourers, jiggers for measuring, corkscrew, bottle and can openers,

ice scoop and tongs, bar napkins, bar towels, ice bins, stir sticks and straws, ashtrays and matches, containers to hold garnishes, bus tubs, trash containers, fruit knife and cutting board.

Miscellaneous items needed:

Juices (tomato, orange, grapefruit, cranberry, pineapple), sour mix, cocktail olives and onions, cherries, lemon and lime wedges, lemon twists, orange slices, Tabasco, Worcestershire sauce, lime juice, grenadine, salt, pepper, and sugar.

14 | *Executing the Function*

The headwaiter (or banquet manager) is in charge of executing the function, coordinating between the service personnel and the requests of the client.

The duties of the headwaiter include:

1. diagraming the place settings according to the number of guests, the size of the tables, and the shape of the location;
2. preparing a schedule of events: introduction, meal, cake ceremony, coffee service;
3. instructing the service personnel in their duties;
4. conducting the ceremonies of the occasion, and controlling the timing of the service;
5. being prepared for cleanup and presentation of the final bill.

The headwaiter must be in charge of the following staff:

Chef: directs kitchen—oversees receipt of food, preparation, plating, and cleanup.

Assistant: receives food, prepares, plates, and cleans under chef's direction; oversees transport.

Helper: helps load and unload food, dishwasher, kitchen prep, setup, and cleaning under assistant's direction.

Driver: loads and unloads food, picks up last-minute items (ice), helps wash dishes, and with setup and

cleaning under assistant's direction; supervises the
outside valet service.

Servers: arrange and drape tables under headwaiter's
direction; set out centerpieces, silverware,
showplates, salt and pepper shakers, and glasses;
serve butler style the hors d'oeuvres during cocktail
hour, clear and clean, and help bartenders; finish
banquet room preparation—water, ice, butter, relish
trays; serve three tables during dinner, except for one
server delegated for the bride's table; and break down
and clean up.

Transportation

Transporting food (even for short distances) takes special
preparation. Most food items should be transported in
either heated or refrigerated containers. Never leave
perishables out at room temperature. The right holding
temperatures are 45° F for cold food, and 140° F for hot food.

Also, don't pack foods tightly in their containers. Allow
air to circulate.

Throw away any food that spills during transport. And
clean the food transport containers after every use with
bleach and hot water.

Banquet Setup

The banquet room is prepared for setup by vacuuming the
rug and/or cleaning the floor. The walls and windows
should also be washed, and anything unsightly should be
covered or removed from the room.

Remember to clean the attendant rooms as well—
restrooms, checkroom, and dressing rooms. It should be the
job of one employee (bar backup or kitchen helper) to check
these rooms periodically throughout the function to make
sure they stay clean.

The banquet room should be completely set up before any of the guests begin to arrive.

Table Layout

To allow comfortable spacing when setting up the tables, leave two and one half feet between the backs of chairs. Service aisles should be slightly larger for the waiters to walk through holding their trays.

The legs of the tables should be positioned squarely to one another, with the drapes covering all four legs evenly. The drape should hang at least sixteen inches to adequately cover the table.

Place Setting

The headwaiter creates a sample place setting for the servers to follow. The average place setting for each person is twenty inches wide.

No more than three types of glasses are set out on the table at any time. The water glass is placed directly above the entrée knife. If the champagne glass is next to be used, it is placed directly to the right of the water glass. The wine glass is then placed above the first two, forming the apex of the triangle.

Napkins can be either the same color as the tablecloth, or contrasting for a more dramatic effect. The napkin is either placed in the wine glass, or folded on the showplate.

The flatware should all be set in place before service begins. The knives and spoons are on the right, and the forks on the left. On both sides, flatware should be set in the order in which it will be used, going from the outside in. For instance, if the first course is a salad, then the salad fork should be placed to the left of the dinner fork. The cutting edges of all knives should face left.

If each waiter sets his own assigned tables, there will be subtle differences between them. Instead, have one waiter set out the glasses, another the flatware, another the napkins and place cards. The final preparations include pouring the water and lighting the candles.

Banquet Service

The quality of service is as important as the quality of the food. As you know from dining in restaurants, the finest meals can be marred by careless or rude service. Your employees must be polite, clean, and ready to inform the guests about the menu and beverages that are being offered.

The headwaiter determines the way the servers perform their duties. The style of service must be uniform in order to convey a seamless presentation. It is more important that all the servers pour water from the same side than worry about which side is "correct." And a certain seat at each table should be designated as the starting point for service.

In sit-down service, the food is usually served pre-plated. The exception is formal service, where each course is served at the table from silver platters. However, most catered functions don't include this type of formal service.

Once the guests have started to arrive, the servers should position themselves around the edge of the room, near their stations. They politely introduce themselves by name to the guests, and wear name tags.

The servers watch the headwaiter, who will signal each stage of the function. The easiest method is to have the headwaiter move to a visible location near the kitchen when it is time to begin serving each course.

The servers should also have a set pickup order in the kitchen, with the waiter for the head table first in line.

Formal Service

Formal service is much more elaborate than the conventional sit-down service. Food is presented on silver trays to each guest, and the waiters must be deft with service spoons and forks or the effect will be awkward.

With formal service, the rules are much stricter. You start serving with the hostess or main guest. Clean, empty plates are placed and removed from the table from the guest's right, in a clockwise rotation around the table. Beverages are also served from the guest's right, in a clockwise rotation.

All the food is served from the guest's left, counterclockwise around the table. The serving utensil is held in the right hand, and the platter or tureen is held in the left. This keeps the server from brushing against the platter with their sleeve.

Ideally, each course should be served from a separate platter, but you can serve the entrée, starch, and vegetable from one large platter if the function is small enough.

When setting the table, the silverware is usually positioned in menu order from the outside (appetizer) to the inside (dessert). With formal service, the entrée knife and fork are placed closest to the showplate and the dessert spoon is placed above the showplate.

Serving the Wine

The first wine, usually a white wine, is served just prior to the appetizer. All of the bottles are opened in the kitchen and carried into the banquet room to be individually served.

The server holds the bottle with a folded service napkin in his right hand, to keep the warmth of his hand away from the chilled wine. The server should not cover the label, which is positioned up so the guests can see it if they wish.

The server pours from the right, starting with the key guest and moving clockwise around the table. Before the function, the servers should be shown the level of the right amount (5 oz.).

As the pouring is completed, the bottle should be twisted gently as it is raised, to prevent dripping. Drips can be wiped from the neck with the service napkin.

After everyone is served, the remaining wine should be returned to ice buckets or the refrigerator to keep it chilled. The glasses are refilled throughout the night until the budgeted amount has been consumed.

Serving the Appetizer

The servers fill their trays with pre-plated appetizers, or soup bowls, or salads. It makes a nice presentation if all of the servers leave the kitchen at the same time so they can all start serving at once.

After the appetizers are served, the waiters return the empty trays to the kitchen and attend to any requests made by the guests. Dirty ashtrays should be cleaned, bread baskets refilled, butter replenished, etc. Water glasses should be refilled, pouring from an iced pitcher directly into the glass while it rests on the table.

The appetizer plates are removed at a signal from the headwaiter. The plates shouldn't be scraped at the table, but stacked with the utensils on the top, cleanest plate. The stacks should be placed on the serving tray and returned to the kitchen.

Serving the Entrée

Plate covers are essential to keep the entrée hot. It also helps stack the required number of meals for each table.

Don't overload the service trays, and don't let the waiters rest the tray on their shoulders. The tray is carried in the left hand, using the right hand to balance it and open doors.

To keep dishes from slipping, put a damp nakpin or cloth down first. Make sure hot and cold dishes aren't next to one another on the tray. And always use a tray stand rather than placing the tray on the table.

When the entrée is served, the gravy boats are also placed on the table. Then the water is replenished and ashtrays are cleaned.

When the entrée plates are removed, all of the silverware (except dessert flatware), gravy boat, bread basket, butter plate, relish tray, and salt and pepper shakers should also be removed. The tray is returned to the kitchen with the dirty dishes, which the server then scrapes, sorting the glassware from the china and flatware.

Use a crumber to clear the table linen of spilled food.

Serving the Dessert

The coffee service must be prepared so the urns are hot and ready to go once the entrée plates have been removed from the tables. Usually coffee and tea are served first, along with the proper silverware, creamers, and sugar bowls.

On a signal from the headwaiter, the pre-plated desserts are placed on trays and served to the guests. The trays are returned to the kitchen, and the waiter refills coffee cups and water glasses.

When the dessert plates are removed, all of the serviceware except for napkins and water glasses should be removed.

Napkins and water glasses are removed only after the guests have left the function. Linen is never removed from the tables within sight of guests.

Leftover Food

A supply of additional food is likely to be left over if there was no spillage or overconsumption.

The leftover portion should be pointed out to the client, indicating that the buffer was intentional. Strictly speaking, all perishable food items belong to the client. It's nice to

provide take-away containers to package the additional food
for members of the host's family to take home.

Leftover cake and dessert can also be individually
wrapped to give away to guests.

Employee Guidelines:

1. Always be polite and attentive to the guests'
   needs and serve with a helpful, friendly
   demeanor.
2. Dress in a clean, neat uniform.
3. Always carry a clean service napkin in your
   hand or over your arm.
4. Do not smoke, eat, or drink in the banquet room.
5. Do not stand or talk to other staff while in the
   banquet room.
6. Never serve an item that you would not eat
   yourself. If the dish's quality or appearance is
   questionable, return it to the kitchen.
7. Know how to explain the food and its
   ingredients to the guests.
8. Ask each guest before removing partially filled
   liquor, wine, beer, or cordial glasses.
9. Keep your area clean and organized, including
   the floors.
10. Carry silverware on top of a folded napkin on a
    plate.
11. Don't put your fingers inside the rims of plates
    when serving.
12. Don't pick up glasses by the rims when removing
    them.
13. Don't stack coffee cups or soup bowls on top of
    one another.

Final Bill

The headwaiter is responsible for presenting the final bill to the client at the conclusion of the function. It's the headwaiter's job to make sure that all of the details specified in the contract have been fulfilled.

The final head count is tallied by the waiters at the beginning of the service, and again after the entrée service to account for late arrivals. These tallies are given to the headwaiter, who will check them against the final guarantee. If the numbers differ more than the percentage stipulated, this should be brought to the attention of the client along with the policy of your business.

The final bill should be prepared by the accounting department, then checked by the headwaiter at the function. Any deviations should be recorded on the final bill, along with any extra charges or rebates.

15 | *Administration*

When you set up your catering kitchen and business office, you must conform to local laws, zoning ordinances, business leases, and contract guidelines. You'll also need the proper licenses, permits, and insurance that are necessary to run a food business.

There are legal and accounting professionals who specialize in the restaurant and catering field. You might find it's worthwhile in the long run to consult with local professionals when you're planning to open a catering business.

Legal

The legal side of the catering business involves insurance, taxes, and laws on the federal, state, and local levels.

Zoning laws need to be observed or you'll receive fines and temporary (or permanent) closure of your business. These laws dictate:

1. type, size, and location of businesses;
2. building and fire codes, inspections, and permits;
3. restrictions as to hours and days of business operation;
4. restrictions as to noise and congestion;
5. storage restrictions;
6. parking restrictions (commercial and private vehicles);

7. sign laws (color, size, height, etc).

You'll also need the necessary license to operate commercial vehicles, and more importantly, to be able to sell food.

The Board of Health grants licenses for varying fees according to the type, size, and location of your business. You must adhere to local sanitation and health regulations. Inspectors will visit your catering kitchen periodically and issue sanitation inspection reports. Violations can result in temporary suspension or revocation of your license.

Liquor License

You must have a liquor license in order to sell liquor. The laws, fees, and requirements vary from state to state, so find out what restrictions apply to off-premises catering.

In order to get a liquor license, you'll have to fill out a detailed application, including:

1. statement of your business (and sometimes personal) finances;
2. whether you are bondable;
3. blueprints of facility (if it's an on-premises facility);
4. conditions of liquor sales;
5. copies of all licenses and permits necessary to conduct ordinary business.

There is a filing fee for the license application, then a fee that is either paid annually or in one lump sum.

The rules and regulations pertaining to your area must be adhered to at every function you cater. In some areas, you need a separate liquor permit for each function, stating the location the liquor will be sold.

Your liquor license can be revoked for the following reasons:

1. false information or omission on the application;

2. conviction for a felony;
3. serving minors;
4. violation of rules and regulations of license;
5. previous suspension or revocation of license.

Accounting

You can also hire an accountant on a consultative basis to help set up your business operations. You need to keep accurate business records, and follow standardized forms. Your business must conform to the Fair Labor Standards Act which establishes minimum wage, overtime pay, and equal pay.

An accountant will also guide you on how to file your taxes and take the benefits and business deductions your business is entitled to. The business must have an identification number for sales and income taxes, and in case of a tax audit, you should have an accountant to represent you.

Aside from the legal aspects of bookkeeping, an accountant can give you sound business advice by analyzing your income and expenses. A profit or loss statement lists your income and deducts your expenses, giving you the net profit or loss for your business. A balance sheet shows your business in terms of assets, liabilities, and net worth. These three markers can tell you exactly where your finances are being apportioned, indicating the areas that need adjusting.

At the same time, an accountant will analyze your payroll and inventory cost as a percentage of your total sales revenue. This can help you determine whether you should buy your baked goods or do your own baking. Or if you should hire a full-time cook or hire kitchen staff on a by-function basis.

Insurance

Whether you're conducting an on- or off-premise catering operation, you need adequate insurance coverage for anything that may happen.

An insurance agent or broker can tell you the types of coverage that are required by state and local laws. You can find out ways of combining insurance policies and reducing the rates by adding health and safety features to your establishment.

In general, you must consider the following insurance:

1. Workers' compensation is paid by the employer, providing employees with reimbursement for medical costs and loss of income arising from an on-the-job injury. Rates are based on the type of jobs in your business, the total amount of payroll dollars, and the number of employees you have. As with any insurance, your premium is lower if you don't have claims filed against your business. You can be insured either through a state insurance fund or, in some states, through private insurance companies. If your business isn't covered, you can be sued by an injured employee.

2. Social Security is retirement insurance paid to the federal government by both the employer and employee. A percentage of the salary (approximately 7 percent) is withheld from each worker's paycheck, and is paid by the employer, along with their percentage contribution.

3. Unemployment insurance is usually granted by the state, and guarantees income for the employee when there is a loss of employment for just cause. This doesn't include employees that you deem unfit for service and must fire. The employer·pays the insurance, which is a percentage of the

payrolls' taxes (varying from state to state).

4. Accident and health insurance is becoming a premium selling point for potential employees. If you can get a good health plan for a low premium, many full-time employees will consider taking a lower salary. This insurance covers employees for illnesses and injuries incurred off the job.

5. General business insurance protects you from most physical property losses from fire, smoke damage, theft, burglary, water leakage and damage, boiler breakdowns, and other property damage. Building insurance can be carried if your business owns the building, and it covers all permanent fixtures: plumbing, elevators, heating and air conditioning units.

6. Comprehensive liability insurance covers any claim a client or guest may have against a caterer for personal or bodily injury incurred on the premises due to neglect. Claims may be due to bodily injury as a result of slipping on a wet floor, tripping on carpeting or steps, or because of faulty lighting. Comprehensive liability insurance can also cover product liability, which are claims due to unsanitary or spoiled food and beverages.

7. Equipment insurance protects against damages to equipment that may be incurred during transport and use. All equipment needs to be listed on the policy in order to be covered.

8. Commercial truck accident insurance covers your transports against any suit involving bodily injury or property damage. You can also get cargo insurance to cover food supplies lost while in transit or unloading. Comprehensive coverage protects the car from loss or physical damage (broken headlight or dent).

16 | *On-Premises Catering*

When your catering business starts going strong, you'll naturally want to expand and open a banquet facility of your own. It makes sense, since all you have to do is pay for a few large, empty rooms (attached to your catering kitchen) and instantly you have added income and complete control over the functions.

You can also rent rooms without providing food or a higher room rental can be charged depending on how little food is ordered. On the other hand, room rentals can also be reduced or eliminated depending on the price of the menu.

Like everything else in catering, when you are looking for your own banquet facility, the most important aspect is its physical attractiveness. Your business must offer something special, so that potential clients will want to hold their most treasured events with you.

Think of your banquet facility as a stage where elaborate productions must be carried out every week. The landscaping, exterior, lighting, and interior decoration should work together to create a pleasing environment, yet be flexible enough to suit each client.

The Building

Often, creating a banquet facility will involve converting an existing structure. Almost any building with a large central room can be used—a theater, car dealership, supermarket, an old school, hotel, or a large house.

The location must be attractive, or your clients will be unimpressed before they even get to your salesperson. Take advantage of a landscape architect in order to get the best layout for your grounds. The lawns, shrubbery, trees, hedges, and flowers will be the first things your clients see when they are approaching your facility.

To separate you from neighboring establishments, erect wrought iron fences and gates, stone walls, columns, and decorative hedging to lend an atmosphere of privacy and distinction. If the location is in a strip mall, shift the entrance from the front to the side (or rear), where special planters and awnings can be placed to form a separate façade for your business.

Your sign should be memorable, incorporating your logo or the tone of your business. If you cater primarily to seminars and trade shows, then your sign and exterior should be professionally correct. If you cater to private parties and formal affairs, the sign and exterior should be discreet and elegant.

Canopies, awnings, and overhangs are essential to protect arriving guests from bad weather. Your main door should have a carpeted entrance and a doorman to help arriving guests.

Parking facilities are important, as well. One parking space should be available for every two to four seats, up to the capacity of your facility. Take into account the need to maintain the asphalt and gravel of your parking lot and driveway. And it would be best to establish your own valet parking.

Garden Area

The outdoor lighting is very important, and if it is flexible enough, it can create the proper mood for any function.

You can hang lanterns from trees or porches, or place decorative lampposts along the pathways. Gardens, benches, and fountains should be carefully lit, to show off your facility to its best advantage. For safety, direct and indirect lighting can illuminate steps, patios, planters, driveways, pathways, and parking areas.

If you have adequate space, consider decorating your grounds with statues, gazebos, or water displays such as fountains, ponds, and waterfalls. You can also build patios or terraces to accommodate outside functions.

One quick way to get your own on-site banquet facility started is to house your catering kitchen on property that is large enough to accommodate outdoor parties. By putting up tents or permanent pavilions, you can create an attractive setting for different types of functions during the warmer months.

With a portable dance floor, you can even offer dancing. Or you can offer outdoor sports, such as croquet, goofy golf, horseshoe pits, volleyball courts, or even a ball field. Special barbecue grills or pits can be installed, and permanent liquor bars can be erected at little additional cost.

The Interior

Your facility should have an entrance area that is large enough to serve as a waiting room for guests arriving and leaving. All-weather carpeting should be put in this area, which creates a buffer zone between the door and the lobby.

The lobby should be large enough to accommodate the total number of guests for each function. Decorate it comfortably with chairs, sofas, tables, and carpeting, so it can serve as a room for the cocktail hour, or as a buffer zone between several different banquet rooms. Public telephones should be placed in the lobby, and your business can make additional money by providing cigarette vending machines.

The checkroom is adjacent to the lobby, and must be large enough to hold the total number of garments of the total number of functions being held at any one time. Quick service is essential when it comes to coat-check. Since your guests arrive and leave in bunches, a wide coat-check with many stations (which can be manned by service personnel before and after the function) is preferable to a deep room with a single person at the counter.

The bathrooms have to conform to certain health codes as far as number, location, and accessibility is concerned. You also need to conform to laws for the physically disabled, ensuring there is wheelchair access. However, extra care in designing and maintaining your bathrooms can give your establishment a luxurious air. Textured wallpaper, excellent lighting, unique fixtures, fresh flowers, and a counter of personal beauty supplies can add the perfect touch to your banquet facility.

Private Rooms

If you cater wedding receptions, you must have a couple of private rooms that can be used as dressing rooms. These rooms can also be used by the host's family at bar mitzvahs, and birthday and anniversary parties. Private rooms also serve as changing rooms for fashion shows or as private meeting rooms.

The private rooms are decorated with sofas, chairs, a desk, dressing and cocktail tables, and should have adjacent rest room facilities. They also have a closet, mirrors, and telephone access.

For a party, you can put a bottle of complimentary champagne on ice in the dressing room, or provide a separate tray of hors d'oeuvres or French pastries. Be sure to have your salesperson point out the advantage of having a private area where the host's family can freshen up and leave their belongings during the party.

Private rooms can also be used as cocktail areas adjoining the banquet rooms. The recommended size for a cocktail area is usually one-third of the banquet room. The bars can be permanently placed in these rooms, which can also be rented out for smaller functions.

Banquet Rooms

The banquet room is the main room of your facility. Banquet rooms can accommodate 50, 75, 100, 125, 150, 200 or more people.

If you have more than one banquet room, and host functions at the same time, the walls of each room must be fairly soundproof to avoid disturbing the other parties. There are companies that specialize in folding doors that are soundproof, and these give the added advantage of being able to subdivide your space for multiple smaller rentals.

The carpeting is also extremely important—it must resist stains, yet elegantly complement your decor. Choose a pattern that will obscure stains, while avoiding a uniformly light color. Large designs or floral patterns are best, in neutral shades with darker elements that can coordinate with the different color schemes of your functions.

The dance floor and bandstands can be either permanent or portable, to allow room rental for other types of functions. Portable dance floors come in sections—four by four or three by six feet—that easily attach together. Or you can snap carpeting over the dance floor when it's not in use.

The dance floor should be at least one-sixth the total size of the room or it will look skimpy. In reality, no more than half of the guests will ever dance at the same time.

The audio systems must be very good or your bands will never sound satisfactory. And lighting is important—rheostats must be on all the switches so you can raise and lower the lights to suit each function.

The Office

The banquet office is a showcase for your business. It is where the salesperson meets with potential clients, and where clients come to sign the contract. It is also where the administrative work takes place, so it must be efficient as well as attractive.

The reception area should have comfortable, attractive seating where clients can wait. You won't need more than six or eight seats. The reception desk can be in the same room, with adjacent doors leading to the interior offices of the salespeople and administrative staff.

Your business brochures should be displayed and readily available for clients to browse through. And prominently display framed photographs of some of your functions, cakes, and special decorations.

Employee Areas

You must be able to store all your equipment when the function rooms are emptied. This includes storage for rented equipment, linen, uniforms, liquor, and cleaning supplies.

Your employees will also need changing rooms, rest rooms, and break rooms where they can relax out of sight of the guests. Make these areas as nice as the guests' areas, and your employees will work for you with respect.

17 | *Functions On-Premises*

Most functions are carried out basically the same way whether you are an on- or off-premises caterer. However, there are two types of functions that you can add to your list of specialties once you have your own banquet facilities—wedding ceremonies and conventions.

Weddings

By offering your banquet facilities to hold the wedding ceremony in the same location as the reception, you attract far more clients, while receiving revenue on chapel rental, rehearsal dinner, and additional flowers, decorations, and music.

You simply need to dedicate one of your smaller banquet rooms as an on-site chapel. An interior decorator can show you how to give the room a joyful, etherial atmosphere. Even a tasteful garden bower can serve as a chapel for spring and summer weddings.

Many clients prefer on-site weddings because it cuts down on travel time and lends unity to their wedding festivities.

Rehearsal

A few days prior to the actual ceremony, the wedding participants are called together for a rehearsal of the ceremony. It is conducted by the banquet manager or the headwaiter, and is usually accompanied by a luncheon or dinner for the entire bridal party. Traditionally, the groom's parents arrange and pay for the rehearsal dinner.

Since the actual ceremony will differ according to religious rituals, it's best to consult with the clergyman prior to the rehearsal to get a basic idea of the proceedings. The clergyman always has the final say as to how the ceremony is conducted. Some clergymen will want to conduct the entire rehearsal and service themselves without the assistance of the banquet manager, while others expect the caterer to organize the entire proceedings.

At the rehearsal, the participants will be shown their positions during the wedding ceremony. Timing and cues for their entry, the rituals of the ceremony, and their exit will also be discussed. If one of the participants is unable to attend, it is up to the client to inform them of their duties.

The headwaiter instructs the participants in the proper forms for the processional. The processional should be conducted at a slow, measured pace, to allow the participants plenty of time to consider every move. Most of all, you don't want your bridal party to look flustered or hurried during the ceremony.

Wedding Ceremony

Set your lobby up as a hospitality room for guests who arrive early for the wedding ceremony. This is particularly appreciated if your banquet facility is located at some distance from the guests' homes. You can offer coffee, tea, juice, Danish, coffee cake, fruit and cookies. It costs very little to do, and creates a nice gratis touch that you can add to the festivities.

Whenever the wedding ceremony is on-site, the banquet manager is responsible for organizing the processional, recessional, and receiving line, as well as the entrance into the reception hall, cutting of the cake, and throwing the bouquet and garter.

Basic Christian Ceremony

The headwaiter instructs the ushers in seating the arriving guests (one usher for every forty guests). The parents, siblings, and grandparents are seated in the first pews. The bride's relatives and guests are seated on the left side, and the groom's are on the right.

After all the guests are seated, an usher escorts the bride's mother down the aisle to the first pew. The guests rise as the clergyman enters (usually from one side) and takes his position at the head of the room. The groom and best man can immediately follow the clergyman, with the groom standing on the left.

Music signals the start of the processional. The ushers can join the groom and best man by entering from the side, by filing down the center aisle, or by walking down in couples with the bridesmaids. The bridesmaids can either enter in pairs or single file, with the maid of honor last. If a ring bearer or flower girl is included, he or she follows next. Usually it's best to let small children sit on the first pew with the family members.

The bride enters holding her father's right arm. Together, they walk down the aisle as the wedding march is played. They pause at the first pew, where the father removes the veil and kisses his daughter.

The groom walks down from the front to meet her. The father steps aside, allowing the groom to offer his right arm to the bride. The couple continues down the aisle, taking their position in front of the clergyman. The father sits in the left front pew next to his wife.

The maid of honor takes the bridal bouquet before the ceremony begins, and assists in arranging the bride's gown. The best man should be ready to offer the rings when asked by the clergyman.

The recessional is conducted in reverse order to the processional, with the bride and groom first, and the paired attendants following. The first pews of family and relatives file out next, with the guests leaving last.

As the bridal party is leaving the chapel, the banquet manager arranges them in the receiving line, directing the rest of the guests along the line and into the cocktail room. The guests can begin their cocktails while the photographs are being taken.

Basic Jewish Ceremony

There are certain ritual items that you will need to have for a Jewish ceremony.

The *chuppah* is a four-posted floral or cloth canopy that covers the ceremony, symbolizing the sanctity of the bridal chamber of the couple. A small table is placed under the chuppah, holding a bottle of kosher wine and two wine glasses. The caterer can either add a white linen napkin (for wrapping the glass) or set out a prewrapped glass. At the conclusion of the ceremony, this glass will be placed on the floor so the groom can break it with the heel of his shoe. Many Judaic-item stores sell special thin-walled glasses that crush more easily than regular glasses.

You should also provide yarmulkes for the male guests. Arrange them on a linen-covered table outside the chapel so the men can place one on their head before entering. At an extra fee, you can provide yarmulkes embroidered with the names of the couple and the date of the wedding.

During the processional, unlike the Christian wedding, the groom's family and friends sit on the left while the bride's sit on the right. The rabbi enters first, either down the center aisle or from one side, taking up his position under the chuppah.

The ushers seat the grandparents in the first pew, then proceed down the aisle in pairs, followed by the best man. They take up position to the left, in front of the chuppah. Next the groom enters with a parent on each side holding his arms. All three proceed down the aisle and stand underneath the chuppah. The groom is closest to the table, facing the rabbi, with the parents at the left side.

The bride's side of the wedding party does exactly the same, with the bridesmaids followed by the maid of honor, then the bride with both her parents. They stop at the first pew, where the groom comes forward to meet them. The bride takes the arm of the groom, and they proceed together under the chuppah. The bride's parents stand to the right of the table, with the bridesmaids in front and to the right.

The recessional leaves in pairs in the following sequence:

1. bride and groom
2. bride's parents
3. groom's parents
4. maid of honor with best man
5. bridesmaids with ushers

Then the grandparents along with the rabbi (and cantor) follow.

Conventions

If you have a large facility, you can also book trade shows and conventions. Your banquet rooms must have high ceilings, good lighting, and plenty of electrical outlets. Create a diagram of every function room that can be utilized, showing the dimensions of the rooms, locations of electrical outlets, doors, and collapsing walls.

When renting space for conventions, you'll have to work closely with the organizers of the function. Cleanup after the show is the caterer's responsibility, so the cost must be calculated into the rental of every room. You must also book a minimum of one hour between functions to clean and reset the room. More formal affairs require more set-up time.

Trade Shows

With trade shows, the promoter sets up the contracts with the individual vendors, and advertises the show. The caterer rents the use of the facility, provides cash bars, coffee service, and food arrangements for the employees of the promoter.

Meetings and Seminars

In order to accommodate meetings and seminars, you'll need additional equipment such as podiums and lecterns. Podiums are free-standing, chest-high rostrums. A lectern is a smaller version that is placed at the head of the table, or on the center of a dias table.

Many companies like to display their logo on the front of the rostrums, but you may permanently place your own logo on your equipment, taking advantage of the free advertising among the participants.

Each room should be supplied with water pitchers and glasses (either on the tables, or at the back of the room), and pens and writing pads. Some clients also request a platform for the speakers' area, and many like to use microphones. Additional audiovisual equipment such as projectors, over-heads, screens, and tape recorders can be rented from outside agencies.

Seating

There are two basic types of seating for meetings: theater and classroom style.

With theater style, the chairs are arranged in lines facing the podium or head table. To estimate the seating capacity of a theater arrangement, divide the square footage of the total seating area by eight. When setting up the rows, leave at least four inches between the chairs, otherwise your attendees will feel hemmed in.

Classroom style seating is used when note-taking is part

of the meeting. To estimate the seating capacity of a classroom style arrangement, divide the square footage of the total seating area by ten. Each person needs two feet of table space—so a six-foot table seats three.

Leave at least thirty inches between conference tables to allow for enough chair room. When setting up the rows, separate tables at least twenty inches apart, and have an aisle for every two tables that is at least forty inches wide.

Whenever you provide tables, cover them with clean linen, or dark green conference cloths. It makes writing easier, and gives the room a polished finish.

18 | *Special Food Preparation*

Since catering is primarily the preparation of food, you should have a few showcase food items to offer your clients. Your chef should be creative in finding recipes that can be prepared for the greatest visual impact.

As one wise caterer once said—even if a guest doesn't like the food, if the presentation looks good he'll say it isn't suited to his taste. But if the food isn't presented in a pleasing manner, the guests will likely say the food is bad.

Food Decoration

Salads can be decorated attractively and used as the focal point of a buffet. Since cold food can stand longer than hot food, you can take more time to garnish and decorate these items.

Arrange trays of petit fours or appetizers in colorful patterns: concentric circles, radial sunbursts, checkered, striped, and patchwork.

Dry food like cookies and hors d'oeuvres should be placed on paper doilies. Sliced meat and cheese should be placed on a bed of lettuce.

Radish roses and other vegetable flowers can also be used as salad garnish. You can also cut designs in vegetables with truffle or chocolate cutters. Decorate meat with fruit patterns (ham decorated with pineapple rings and cherries).

Edible Centerpieces

Edible centerpieces are considered part of the menu since they will be eaten by the guests. You must be sure there is enough of the centerpiece to serve all of the guests, or it is considered decorative and should not be eaten at all (such as a cornucopia of fruit and flowers). Some examples of edible centerpieces include: a large lobster filled with shellfish salad, hams decorated like birds, or a whole fish, turkey, or chicken served on a platter.

Kosher Preparation

Jewish clients will either want glatt kosher or kosher-style (nonkosher) food depending on their observance of religious beliefs. If your business decides to serve kosher food, you must make sure your preparations conform to the dietary laws. That's what kosher means—food that is guaranteed fit and proper to eat by a rabbi.

Kosher caterers must also obey the rule that no food can be cooked or even heated on the sabbath, which begins at dusk on Friday and ends after sundown on Saturday. However, cold foods may be prepared.

You must make sure your premises are absolutely clean to prevent mixing meat and blood, or meat and milk products. Work surfaces should be covered with paper, cooking pots should be dedicated to the type of food they cook, and even the interior of your oven needs to be sterilized after each use.

Since the preparation of kosher meals entails more time and expense, many caterers charge an additional fee per person. Or you can charge a flat rate fee—such as $200 for kosher preparation.

Dietary Law

Always look for a kosher certification to make sure the food you purchase has been inspected. The Union of

Orthodox Jewish Congregations of America puts a circled U on the products they deem kosher.

For meat to be kosher, that means it has been slaughtered under certain conditions. Any animal that dies naturally, or has been killed by wild animals, is considered impure.

There can be no blood in the meat during cooking, so meat tends to come from cuts of the forequarters, rather than the hindquarters which are rich in blood vessels. The meat and fowl must be soaked and salted to ensure all of the blood has been removed.

All pork products are considered nonkosher, including bacon, ham, sausage, and pork chops. An identification tag (a plumba) is attached to the wing of fowls that are considered kosher.

With fish, you don't have to remove all the blood. However, only fish with scales that can be easily scraped off are considered kosher, such as: herring, halibut, bluefish, salmon, whitefish, and tuna. Fish such as eels, sharks, and catfish, and mammals such as dolphins and whales are nonkosher. Shellfish are also nonkosher, such as: shrimp, lobster, mussels, clams, oysters, crabs, and scallops.

Cheese must be certified as kosher by inspectors, as well. Even alcohol based on wine products must be kosher, such as: champagne, vermouth, cordials, and fruit liqueurs. Liquor distilled from grain and cereals is kosher except during religious holidays.

Meat and Milk

You cannot use both meat and milk products in the same meal. Separate sets of dishes, cookware, and flatware must be used, and a distinct interval must pass after meat is consumed before dairy can be eaten. Milk products and meat aren't supposed to come in contact with each other even in the refrigerator, or be cooked close together in the oven.

If meat is served as the entrée, you can't serve butter, milk, or cream with coffee and dessert. However, there are many nondairy products that are called "parve." Eggs are considered parve (unless there's a blood spot inside) and can be eaten with dairy or meat meals.

19 | Kelly's Favorite Recipes

Savannah Planter's Punch

This is a simple yet delicious drink that can be served as a cocktail at parties, dinners, lunches, and brunches.

    6 ounces Jamaican rum
    3 ounces cognac
    1 ounce fresh pineapple juice
    1 lime
    Pineapple, cherry, or sliver of orange for garnish

Mix the rum, cognac, and pineapple juice. Squeeze the lime and add the juice to the mixture.

Chill the glasses, then pack them with crushed ice. Pour the mixture over the ice and stir with a long swizzle stick. Garnish with a ring of pineapple, a cherry, or a sliver of orange.

Serves 2 (multiply by number of guests)

Cascadilla

This chilled, creamy tomato soup is quick to make and is a good accompaniment to lunch and dinner at all times of the year.

    4 cups tomato juice
    1 cup yogurt
    1 chopped cucumber

1 chopped sweet pepper
3 fresh mushrooms, thinly sliced
1 chopped scallion
1 clove crushed garlic
1 teaspoon honey
1/2 teaspoon dill weed
dash of pepper and salt
Croutons
Watercress for garnish

Stir chilled tomato juice and yogurt together. Mix in cucumber, pepper, mushrooms, scallion, garlic, honey, and dill weed.

Serve chilled in bowls, with croutons. Garnish with watercress.

Serves 6

SALAD NIÇOISE

This crunchy tuna and potato salad is a classic, and makes a fine summer dish.

8 new potatoes, about 1 pound, well scrubbed
2 pounds green beans, cooked
10 ripe Italian plum tomatoes, washed and quartered
1 small purple onion, peeled and thinly sliced
1/2 cup Niçoise olives
1/4 cup chopped Italian parsley
pinch of salt
1 teaspoon freshly ground black pepper
1 hard-boiled eggs, shelled and quartered
12 ounce can oil-packed white tuna, drained
3/4 cup vinaigrette dressing

Cook potatoes in boiling salted water until they are tender but not mushy, approximately 10 minutes. Let cool, then cut them into quarters.

Add green beans, tomatoes, onion, olives, parsley, and
the salt and pepper. Pour ½ cup of the vinaigrette over
the vegetables and toss gently but thoroughly.

Transfer mixture to a large serving platter. Arrange the
hard-cooked egg quarters around the edge of the platter.
Flake the tuna over the salad. Drizzle the remaining
vinaigrette and serve at room temperature.

Serves 8

Vegetable Stroganoff

This sour cream and wine sauce is served over vegetables
over flat egg noodles.

1 cup chopped onion
½ pound chopped mushrooms
1 tablespoons butter
3 cups sour cream
1 ½ cups yogurt
3 tablespoons dry red wine
¾ teaspoon salt
¼ teaspoon dill weed
¼ teaspoon black pepper
6 cups of chopped vegetables (broccoli, cauliflower,
    carrots, celery, zucchini, cabbage, yellow peppers,
    and cherry tomatoes)
4 cups flat egg noodles
Scallions, freshly minced, for garnish

Sauté the onions and mushrooms in the butter until
onions are soft. Combine with sour cream, yogurt, red
wine, and spices in the top of a double boiler and gently
heat for 30 minutes.

Steam the vegetables.

Cook the egg noodles in boiling salted water until

tender; drain and butter. Place the noodles in a shallow "bowl shape" on a serving plate, then add the steamed mixed vegetables. Pour the sauce over vegetables and noodles. Garnish with freshly minced scallions.

Serves 6

ROSEMARY LEMON CHICKEN

This entrée is best served with a pasta dish and green salad. It is impressive with its subtle flavoring.

  1 large roasting chicken, about 6 pounds
  4 garlic cloves, peeled and crushed
  5 fresh rosemary sprigs, or 1 tablespoon dried
     rosemary, crushed
  1 lemon
  coarse salt
  lemon slices, for garnish

Preheat oven to 400° F.
Wash and dry the chicken, then rub the garlic cloves and the rosemary over the outside of the bird and in the cavity. Slip one garlic clove and one rosemary sprig under the skin of each breast. Then place the leftover rosemary inside the cavity. Squeeze ½ lemon over the bird and place ½ inside the cavity. Rub salt over the bird and sprinkle inside the cavity.

Place the bird on a shallow rack, breast up, in a roasting pan. Roast it in the oven for 1 to 1 ½ hours, or until the juices run clear, basting once or twice.

Serve hot, carved at the meat station or just prior to service. Or, chill the bird to room temperature and carve on to a platter. Garnish with rosemary sprigs and lemon wedges.

Serves 6

CHOCOLATE MOUSSE

For a chocolate-lover's dessert, the best choice for pretty plating and easy service is chocolate mousse.

1 1/2 pounds semisweet chocolate chips.
1/2 cup prepared espresso coffee
1/2 cup Grand Marnier
4 egg yolks
1 cup heavy cream, chilled
1/4 cup granulated sugar
8 egg whites
pinch of salt
1/2 teaspoon vanilla extract
Candied rosebud, butterfly, or whipped cream for
    garnish

Melt the chocolate chips in a double boiler over very low heat, stirring. Add the espresso, then stir in the Grand Marnier. Let it cool to room temperature, then add the egg yolks to the mixture one at a time, beating each one in thoroughly. Set aside.

Whip the cream until it is thickened, then gradually beat in the sugar. In a separate bowl, beat the egg whites with the salt until they are stiff. Gently fold the egg whites into the whipped cream.

Stir about 1/3 of the whipped cream and egg mixture thoroughly into the chocolate mixture. Then scrape the remaining cream and egg mixture over the lightened chocolate base and fold together gently. Pour into individual dessert cups or serving bowls. Refrigerate for 2 hours, or until set.

Serves 8

Index